MW01067421

Shop Drawings of Shaker Furniture & Woodenware

Volumes 1, 2 & 3

Ejner Handberg

THE COUNTRYMAN PRESS
A division of W. W. Norton & Company
Independent Publishers Since 1923

For information about permission to reproduce selections from
this book, write to Permissions, The Countryman Press, 500
Fifth Avenue, New York, NY 10110

For information about special discounts for bulk purchases,
please contact W. W. Norton Special Sales at specialsales@
wwnorton.com or 800-233-4830

Library of Congress No. 73-83797

Jacket design by Deborah Fillion
Jacket photo by Rick Mastelli/Image & Word

The Countryman Press
www.countrymanpress.com

A division of W. W. Norton & Company, Inc.,
500 Fifth Avenue, New York, NY 10110
www.wwnorton.com

ISBN 978-0-88150-777-5

10 9 8 7 6 5 4

Shop Drawings of Shaker Furniture and Woodenware

Volume 1

Measured Drawings
by Ejner Handberg

PREFACE

This is not an attempt to write a book about the Shakers and their furniture. There are already excellent books which serve that purpose. I refer especially to those by Dr. and Mrs. Edward Deming Andrews. Rather, this is a collection of measured drawings made to scale and with dimensions and details accurately copied from Shaker pieces which have been in my shop for restoration or reproduction. These drawings and patterns have been accumulated over a period of many years of interest in the woodwork of the New England and New York State Shakers.

E.H.
1973

FOREWORD

Ejner (pronounced Eye' ner) Handberg was born in Viborg, Denmark, in 1902. When he was seventeen, he moved to New York. For most of his life, Ejner was a builder in Berkshire County, Massachusetts.

His interest in working with wood began in boyhood on his way to school, when every day he passed a shop where a man worked at a lathe in the window. One of his first jobs as a young man was building lead-lined shipping crates for a Danish firm in New York that made blueprint paper. As a builder, he was perhaps best known for his addition to the handsome old Congregational Church in Stockbridge, and for the studio in the same town that he built for Norman Rockwell in a carriage shed that had been stripped down to the frame.

Building was a way to make a living, according to his wife Elsie, but Ejner's real love was cabinetwork. In 1960, the Handbergs built the Pinewood Shop on Route 102 in Lee, not far from Stockbridge, with a large workshop for Ejner and a gift shop, where Elsie, who was skilled in sewing, offered things that they made.

Ejner's involvement with Shaker furniture began with a chance meeting with Faith and Edward Deming Andrews, noted authorities on the Shakers and residents of nearby Pittsfield. In search of a good cabinetmaker to repair Shaker pieces and a good seamstress for a sewing project, Dr. and Mrs. Andrews had been told of a husband and wife in Lee with those talents. They showed up at the Handberg shop, and in spite of the fact that it was not the Handbergs for whom the Andrewses had been looking, the two couples hit it off.

The visit was the beginning of a friendship as well as a working relationship. The Andrewses often stopped by on Saturdays for tea and something Faith had baked, frequently bringing Shaker furniture items for repair. In the course of his work, and to satisfy his own interest, Ejner began to make lifesize measured drawings of the pieces he handled, scouting the local dump for large refrigerator and stove cartons to get cardboard big enough for his work. In time, a thick stack of drawings accumulated.

Dr. and Mrs. Andrews, who appreciated the kind of understanding that results from the careful examination necessary to produce accurate drawings, urged the Handbergs to publish Ejner's work. The first book, published in 1973, by Berkshire Traveller Press was a family effort. Ejner redrew the pieces to a smaller scale, Elsie did the writing, and their daughter Anne typed the manuscript. Ejner and Elsie collaborated on the four Shaker books that followed, and a last book on measured drawings of 18th-century American furniture in 1983. Ejner died two years later.

Ejner Handberg's books have sold more widely than perhaps any other books on the Shakers. A large part of their appeal is their practical nature and their utter lack of pretense – both, characteristics of Shaker work as well. Did Ejner appreciate the visual kinship between Shaker furniture and contemporary Danish design? No, says Elsie Handberg, adding that her husband didn't even like Danish Modern. Did the Handbergs develop a friendship with the few Shakers who remained at Hancock, Massachusetts, or New Lebanon, New York, as the Andrewses had? No, they didn't; Shaker furniture appealed to them in a way that the Shakers' way of life did not.

Today, Ejner Handberg's straightforward look at Shaker work continues to draw admirers into the Shaker sphere. I am grateful to Elsie Handberg and Anne Handberg Oppermann for insights and reminiscences.

June Sprigg, Curator
Hancock Shaker Village
Pittsfield, Massachusetts
1991

SHAKER REWARD OF MERIT

This Shaker reward of Merit was given to a young Shaker School boy of Hancock, Massachusetts during the nineteenth century. The drawings depict Shakers at work and play during two seasons.

It reads as follows:

The bearer Mr. Elijah Barker receives this as a token of the praise he merits. For his faithfulness and good behavier in schools from his teacher. S.A.P.

Reward of Merit
In the Shaker Manner
to Ejner Handberg
from Faith Andrews

Pittsfield, Mass.   May 1, 1972

*An expression of thanks for your understanding
and appreciation of Shaker furniture.*

*Collectors of this furniture are indeed fortunate
to know of your work and have benefited by your
advice and help.*

*When a restored piece leaves your shop to take
its place in the "world" one is reminded of the
virtues of the early Believers. Honesty, simplicity
and humility were their guiding principles.
When these are adapted by an artisan today we
approach perfection in workmanship.*

F.A.

The late Faith and Edward Deming Andrews devoted decades
of their lives to Shaker research and wrote several
definitive books on the Shakers. Much of their collection
of Shaker artifacts now resides in various museums in
the country and abroad.

CONTENTS

White pine was the most common wood used for furniture like cupboards, chests of drawers, benches, woodboxes and many other items.

Bedposts, chairposts and all parts requiring strength were usually made of hard maple or yellow birch.

Maple, birch and cherry were used for legs on trestle tables, drop leaf tables and stands. The tops were often pine. Square legs are tapered on the inner surfaces only.

Sometimes candlestands, work stands and sewing stands were made entirely of cherry, maple or birch. The legs are dovetailed to the shaft and the grain should run as nearly parallel to the general direction of the leg as possible. A thin metal plate should be fastened to the underside of the shaft and extend about three quarters of an inch along the base of each leg with a screw or nail put in the leg to keep them from spreading.

Parts for chairs and stools were mostly hard maple with an occasional chair made of curly or bird's-eye maple. Birch, cherry and butternut were used less often.

Oval boxes and carriers were nearly always made of maple. The bottoms and covers were fitted with quarter-sawn, edge-grain pine which is less apt to cup or warp than flat-grained boards. First the "fingers" or "lappers" are cut on the maple bands, then they are steamed and wrapped around an oval form and the fingers fastened with small copper or iron rivets (tacks). After they are dry and sanded the pine disks are fitted into the bottom and cover and fastened with small square copper or iron brads.

In New York State and New England, the woods used for the many different small pieces of cabinet work and woodenware were white pine, maple, cherry, yellow birch, butternut and native walnut. They were often finished with a coat of thin paint, or stained and varnished, or sometimes left with a natural finish.

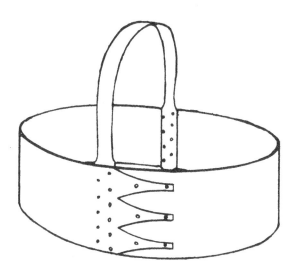

" THAT WHICH HAS IN ITSELF THE HIGHEST USE
POSSESSES THE GREATEST BEAUTY"

PINE CUPBOARD.

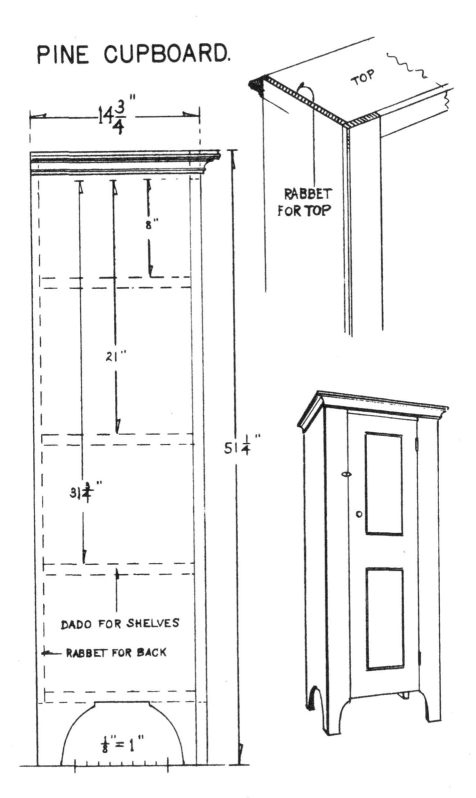

$14\frac{3}{4}$"

8"

21"

$31\frac{3}{4}$"

$51\frac{1}{4}$"

DADO FOR SHELVES

RABBET FOR BACK

$\frac{1}{8}$" = 1"

RABBET
FOR TOP

TOP

PINE CUPBOARD.

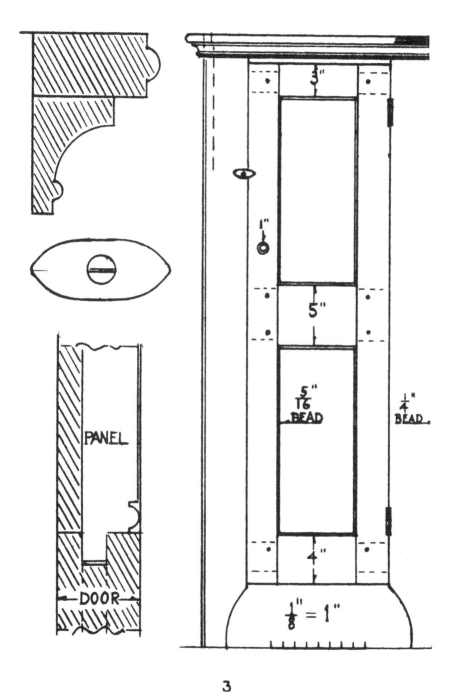

PANEL

DOOR

3"

1"

5"

$\frac{5}{16}$"
BEAD

$\frac{1}{4}$"
BEAD.

4"

$\frac{1}{8}$" = 1"

BED

MAPLE AND WHITEWOOD

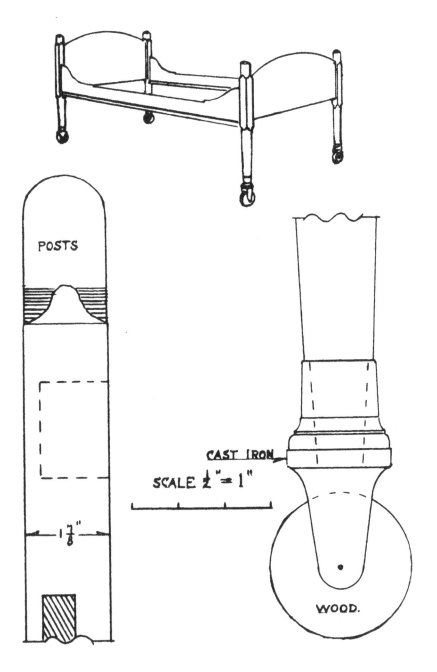

POSTS

CAST IRON

SCALE $\frac{1}{2}'' = 1''$

$1\frac{7}{8}''$

WOOD.

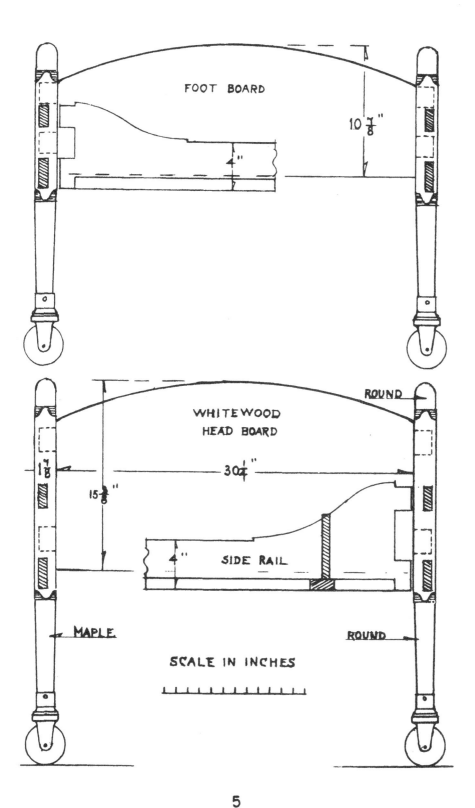

FOOT BOARD

$10\frac{7}{8}$"

4"

WHITEWOOD
HEAD BOARD

$30\frac{1}{4}$"

$1\frac{7}{8}$"

$15\frac{7}{8}$"

ROUND

4"

SIDE RAIL

MAPLE

ROUND

SCALE IN INCHES

5

SEWING DESK

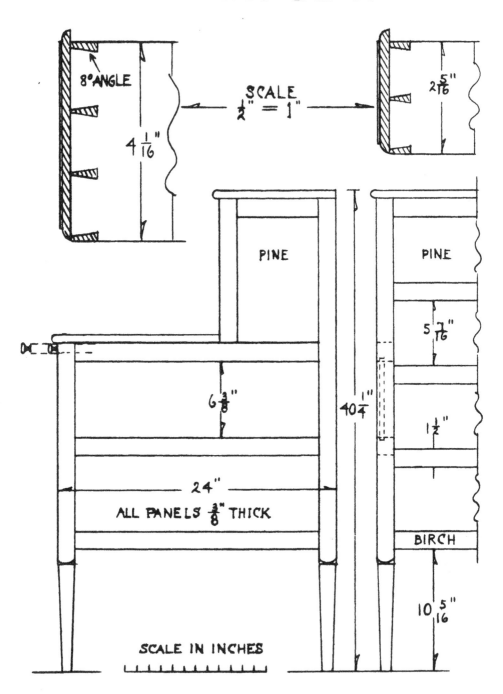

8°ANGLE

$4\frac{1}{16}$"

$2\frac{5}{16}$"

SCALE
$\frac{1}{2}$" = 1"

PINE

PINE

$6\frac{3}{8}$"

$5\frac{7}{16}$"

$40\frac{1}{4}$"

$1\frac{1}{2}$"

24"

ALL PANELS $\frac{3}{8}$" THICK

BIRCH

$10\frac{5}{16}$"

SCALE IN INCHES

SEWING DESK

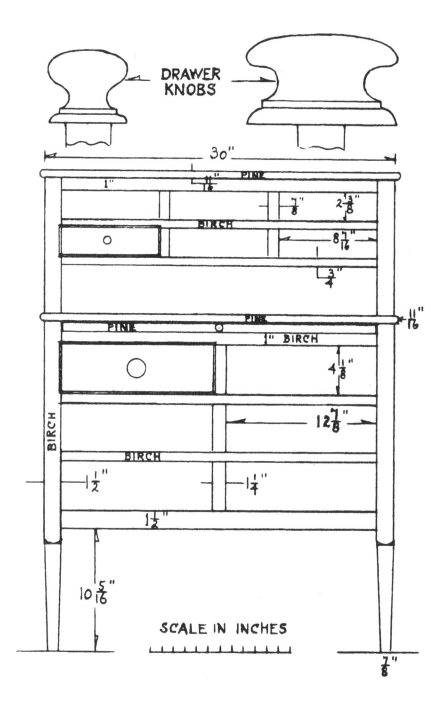

DRAWER KNOBS

30"

PINE

1"

$2\frac{1}{8}"$

$\frac{7}{8}"$

BIRCH

$8\frac{7}{16}"$

$\frac{3}{4}"$

$\frac{11}{16}"$

PINE

PINE

1" BIRCH

$4\frac{1}{8}"$

BIRCH

$12\frac{7}{8}"$

BIRCH

$1\frac{1}{2}"$

$1\frac{1}{4}"$

$1\frac{1}{2}"$

$10\frac{5}{16}"$

SCALE IN INCHES

$\frac{7}{8}"$

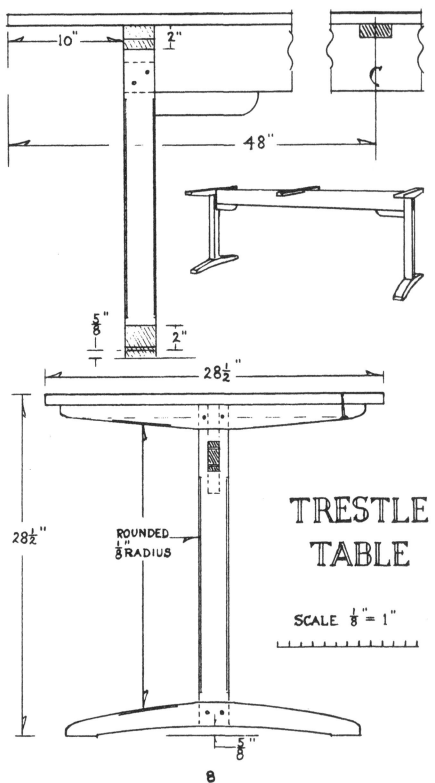

10"

2"

48"

C

5/8"

2"

28 1/2"

28 1/2"

ROUNDED
1/8" RADIUS

5/8"

TRESTLE
TABLE

SCALE 1/8" = 1"

B

TRESTLE TABLE

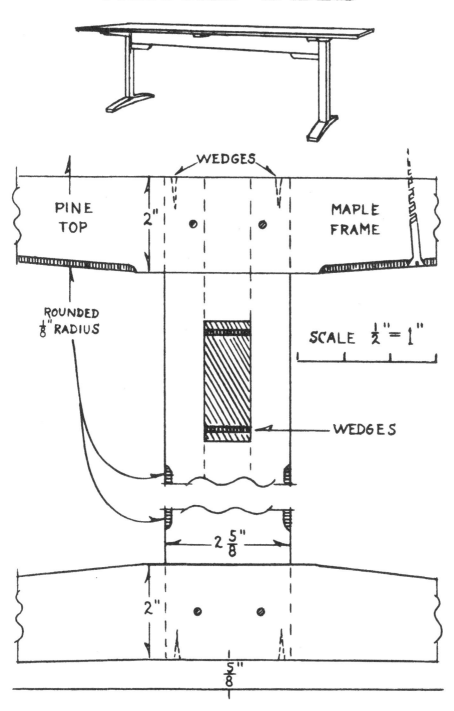

WEDGES

PINE TOP

MAPLE FRAME

2"

ROUNDED $\frac{1}{8}$" RADIUS

SCALE $\frac{1}{2}$" = 1"

WEDGES

$2\frac{5}{8}$"

2"

$\frac{5}{8}$"

SEWING TABLE.

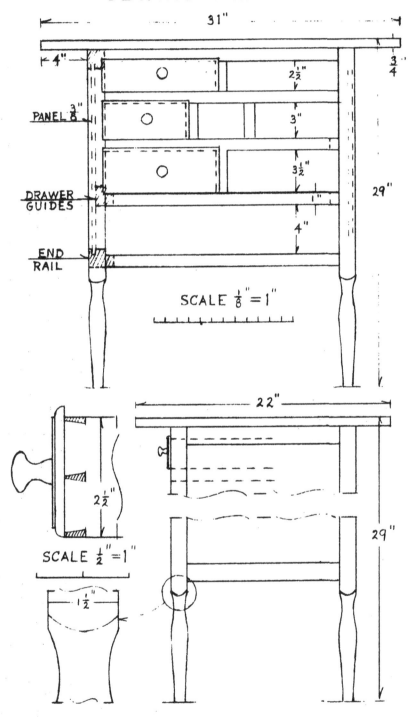

31"

4"

PANEL 3/8"

DRAWER
GUIDES

END
RAIL

2½"

3"

3½"

1"

4"

3/4

29"

SCALE ⅛" = 1"

2½"

SCALE ½" = 1"

22"

29"

1½"

10

WORK TABLE.

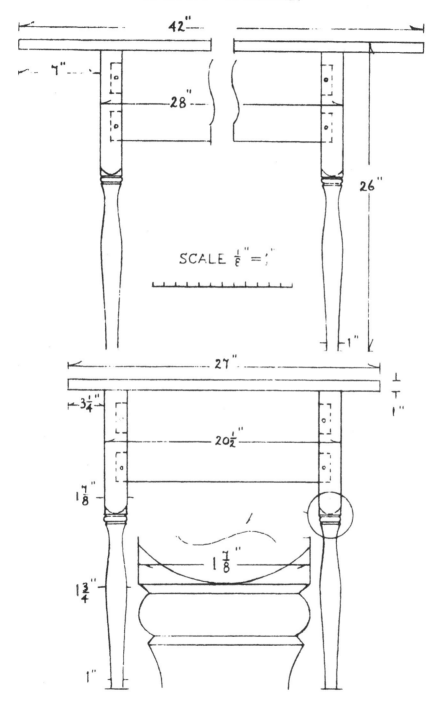

SCALE $\frac{1}{8}" = 1'$

42"

7"

28"

26"

1"

27"

$3\frac{1}{4}"$

$20\frac{1}{2}"$

1"

$1\frac{7}{8}"$

$1\frac{7}{8}"$

$1\frac{3}{4}"$

1"

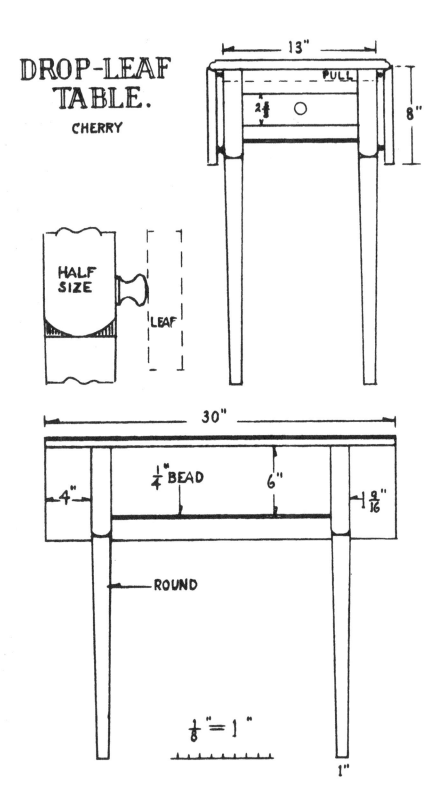

DROP-LEAF TABLE.

CHERRY

13"

PULL

2⅜

8"

HALF SIZE

LEAF

30"

¼" BEAD

6"

4"

1 9/16"

ROUND

⅛" = 1"

1"

DROP-LEAF
TABLE

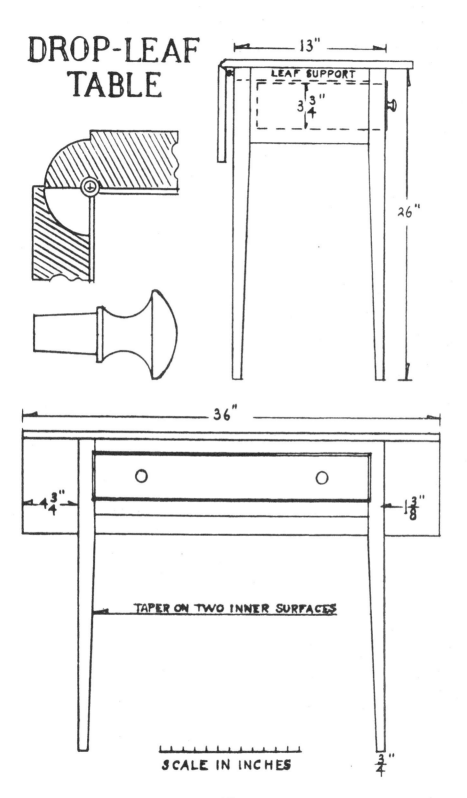

13″

LEAF SUPPORT

$3\frac{3}{4}$″

26″

36″

$4\frac{3}{4}$″

$1\frac{3}{8}$″

TAPER ON TWO INNER SURFACES

SCALE IN INCHES

$\frac{3}{4}$″

13

SEWING STAND.

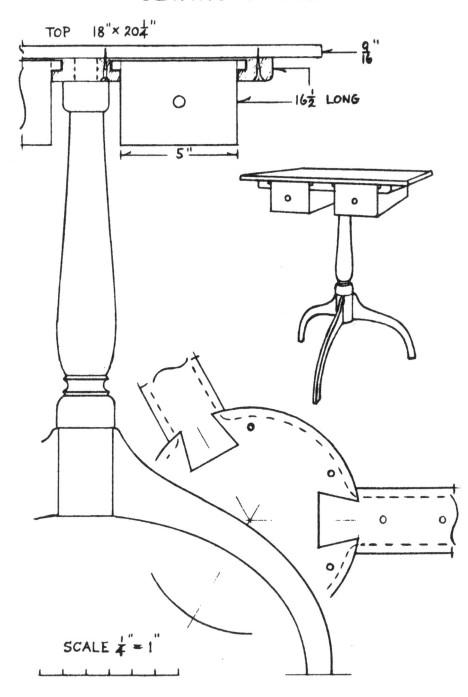

TOP 18" × 20$\frac{1}{4}$"

$\frac{9}{16}$"

16$\frac{1}{2}$ LONG

5"

SCALE $\frac{1}{4}$" = 1"

14

WORKSTAND.

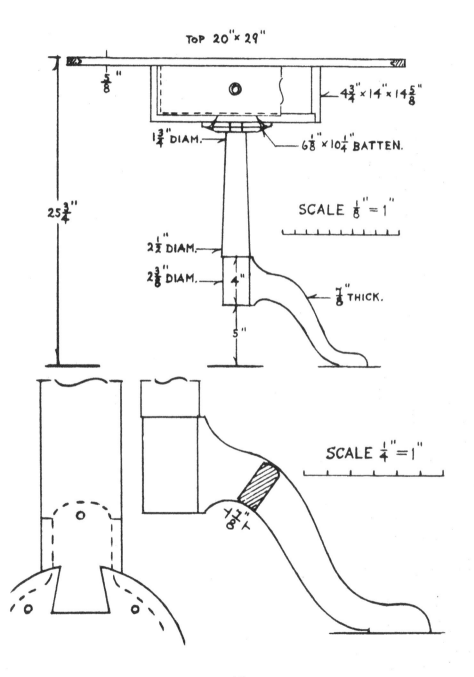

TOP 20" × 29"

$\frac{5}{8}$"

$4\frac{3}{4}$" × 14" × 14$\frac{5}{8}$"

1$\frac{3}{4}$" DIAM.

6$\frac{1}{8}$" × 10$\frac{1}{4}$" BATTEN.

25$\frac{3}{4}$"

SCALE $\frac{1}{8}$" = 1"

2$\frac{1}{2}$" DIAM.

2$\frac{3}{8}$" DIAM.

4"

$\frac{7}{8}$" THICK.

5"

SCALE $\frac{1}{4}$" = 1"

$\frac{7}{8}$"×

15

PEG-LEG STAND.

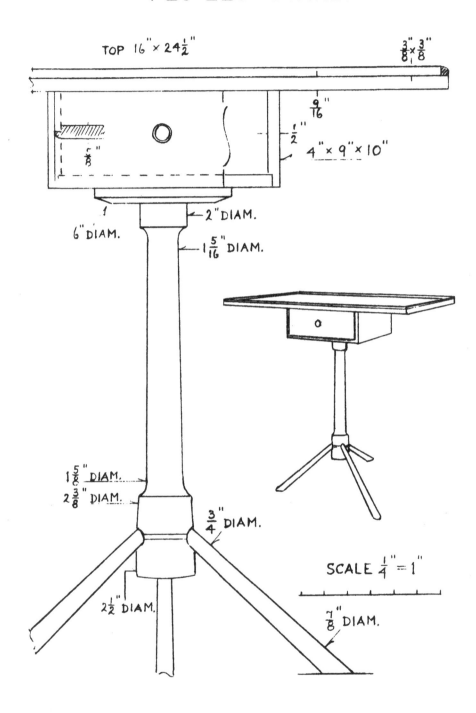

TOP 16" × 24½"

$\frac{3}{8}$" × $\frac{3}{8}$"

$\frac{9}{16}$"

$\frac{1}{2}$"

4" × 9" × 10"

$\frac{5}{8}$"

2" DIAM.

6" DIAM.

$1\frac{5}{16}$" DIAM.

$1\frac{5}{8}$" DIAM.

$2\frac{3}{8}$" DIAM.

$\frac{3}{4}$" DIAM.

$2\frac{1}{2}$" DIAM.

$\frac{7}{8}$" DIAM.

SCALE $\frac{1}{4}$" = 1"

CANDLESTAND.

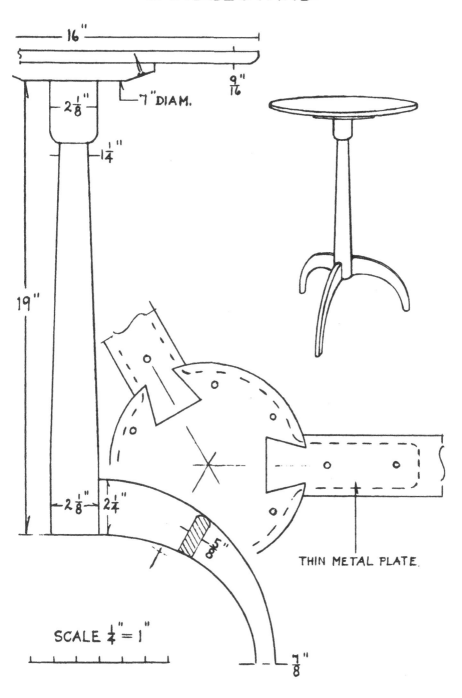

16"

$\frac{9}{16}$"

$2\frac{1}{8}$"

7"DIAM.

$1\frac{1}{4}$"

19"

$2\frac{1}{8}$" $2\frac{1}{4}$"

$\frac{5}{16}$"

THIN METAL PLATE.

SCALE $\frac{1}{4}$"= 1"

$\frac{7}{8}$"

17

TOWEL RACK.

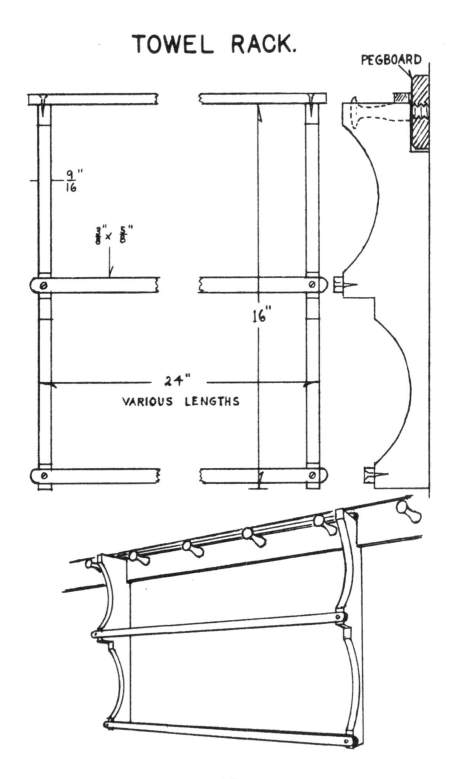

PEGBOARD

$\frac{9}{16}''$

$\frac{3}{8}'' \times \frac{5}{8}''$

16"

24"

VARIOUS LENGTHS

PINE TOWEL RACK

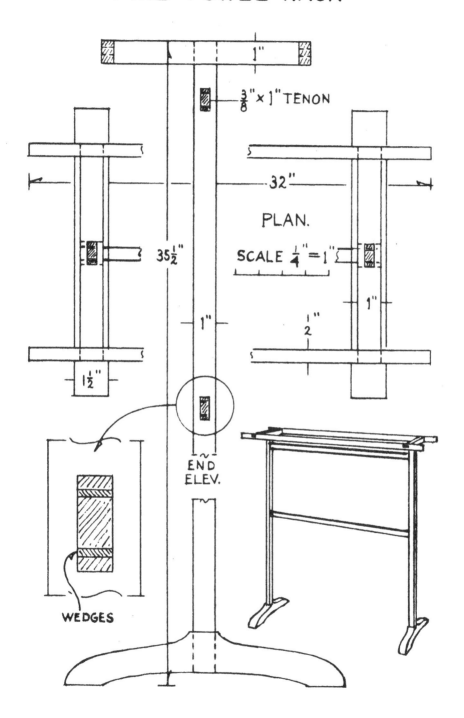

PLAN.

SCALE $\frac{1}{4}'' = 1''$

$\frac{3}{8}'' \times 1''$ TENON

32"

35½"

1"

1"

$\frac{1}{2}''$

1"

1½"

END
ELEV.

WEDGES

LOOKING GLASS.

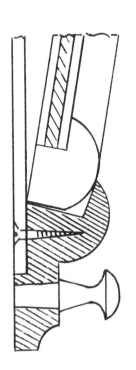

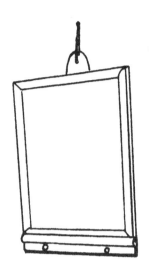

SCALE $\frac{3}{16}$" = 1"

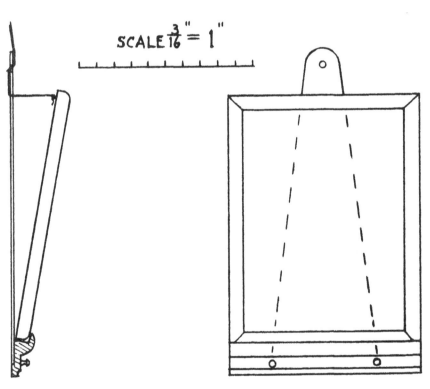

LOOKING GLASS.

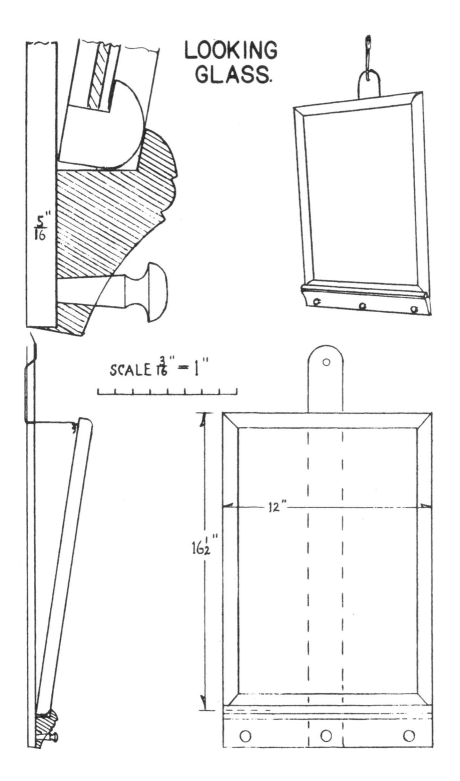

$\frac{5}{16}''$

SCALE $\mathsf{I}\frac{3}{16}'' = 1''$

$12''$

$16\frac{1}{2}''$

21

TABLE -DESK.

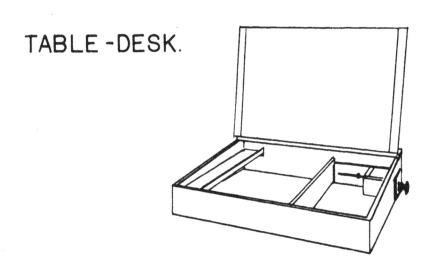

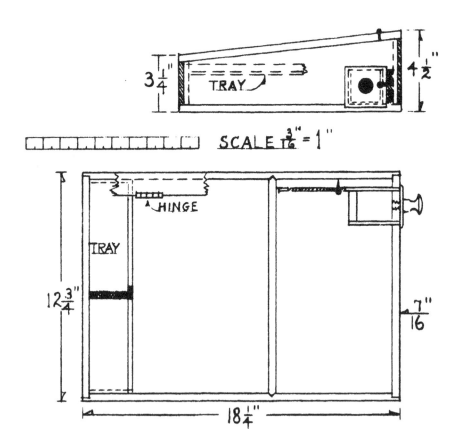

$3\frac{1}{4}''$

TRAY

$4\frac{1}{2}''$

SCALE $1\frac{3}{16}'' = 1''$

HINGE

TRAY

$12\frac{3}{4}''$

$\frac{7''}{16}$

$18\frac{1}{4}''$

TABLE -DESK.
CHERRY AND PINE

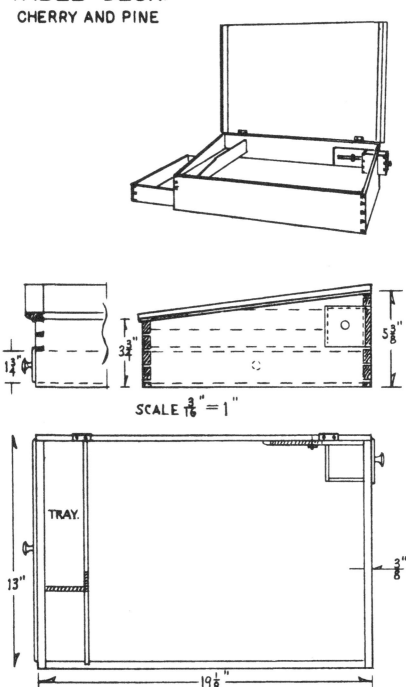

SCALE $\frac{3}{16}" = 1"$

$5\frac{3}{8}"$

$3\frac{3}{4}"$

$1\frac{3}{4}"$

TRAY.

$\frac{3}{8}"$

13"

$19\frac{1}{8}"$

23

KNOBS AND PULLS.

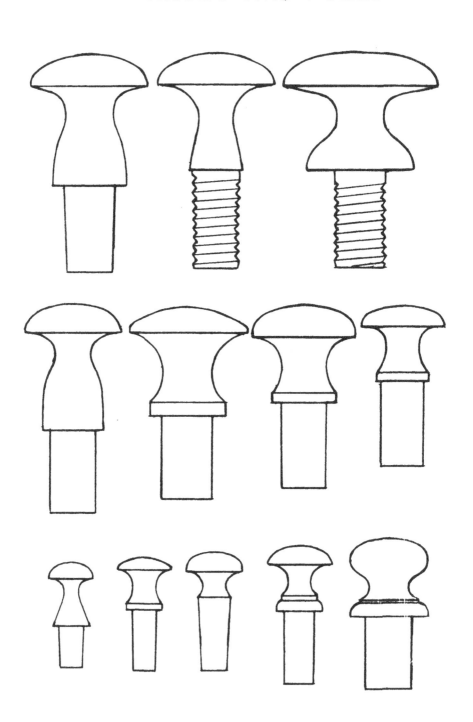

WALL-PEGS.

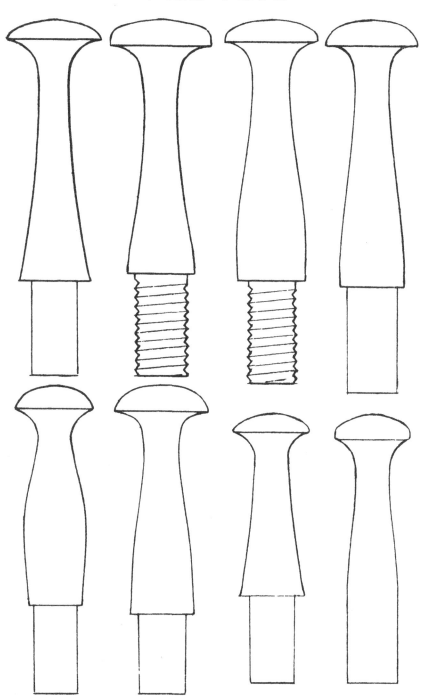

SMALL BENCH.

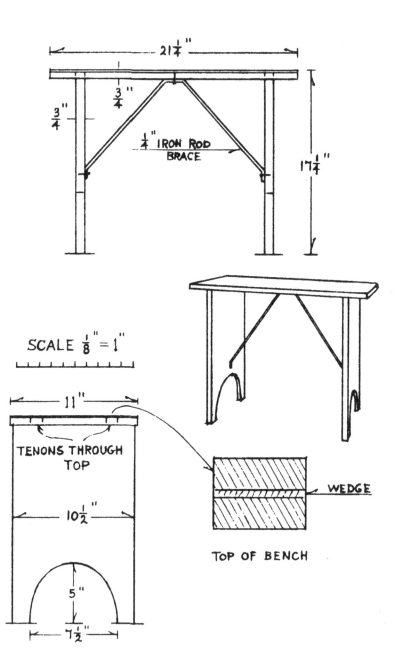

$21\frac{1}{4}$"

$\frac{3}{4}$"

$\frac{3}{4}$"

$\frac{1}{4}$" IRON ROD
BRACE

$17\frac{1}{4}$"

SCALE $\frac{1}{8}$" = 1"

11"

TENONS THROUGH
TOP

$10\frac{1}{2}$"

5"

$7\frac{1}{2}$"

WEDGE

TOP OF BENCH

PINE BENCH.

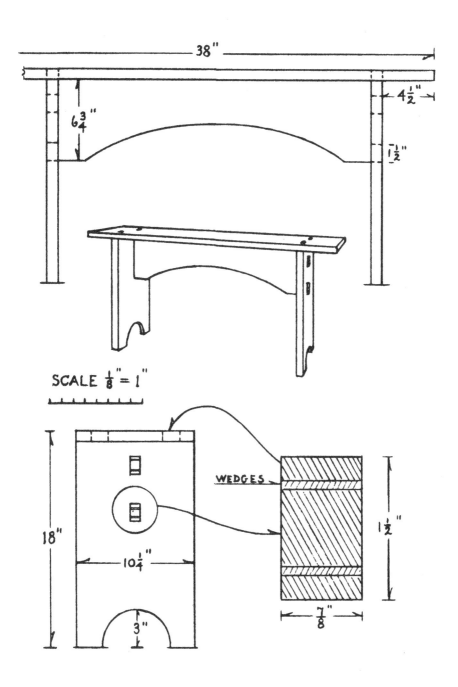

SCALE $\frac{1}{8}'' = 1''$

WEDGES

FOOT BENCHES.

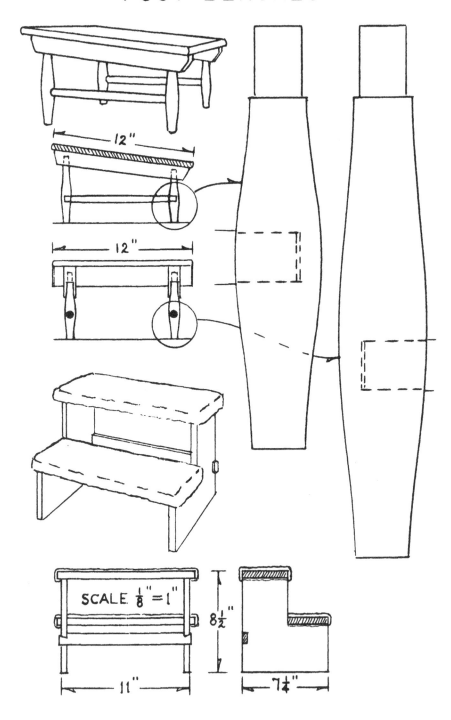

12″

12″

SCALE. $\frac{1}{8}″ = 1″$

$8\frac{1}{2}″$

11″

$7\frac{1}{4}″$

28

FOOTSTOOLS.

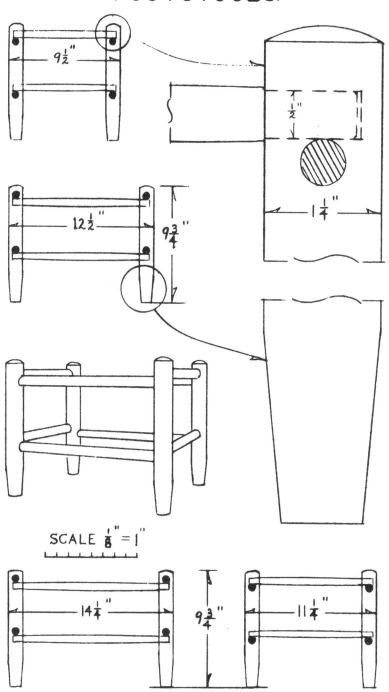

SCALE $\frac{1}{8}$" = 1"

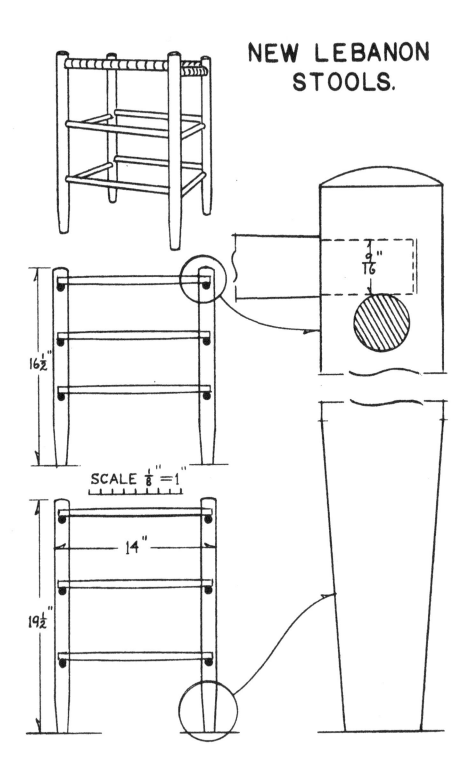

NEW LEBANON STOOLS.

$16\frac{1}{2}''$

SCALE $\frac{1}{8}'' = 1''$

$\frac{9}{16}''$

$14''$

$19\frac{1}{2}''$

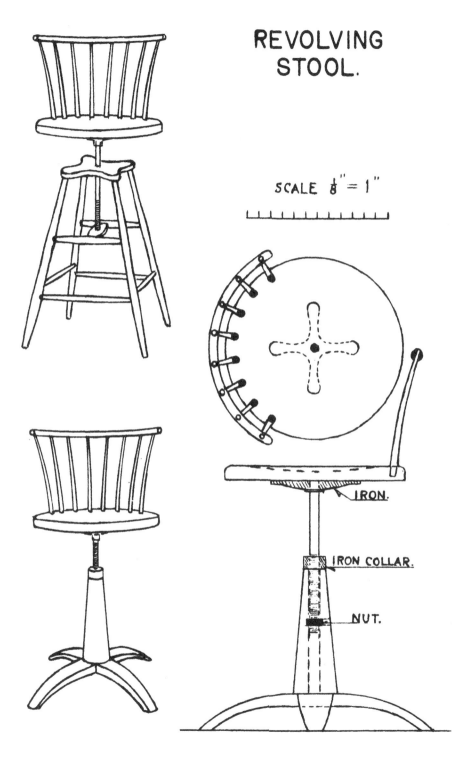

REVOLVING STOOL.

SCALE $\frac{1}{8}'' = 1''$

IRON.

IRON COLLAR.

NUT.

CHILD'S
BENT-WOOD
ROCKER.

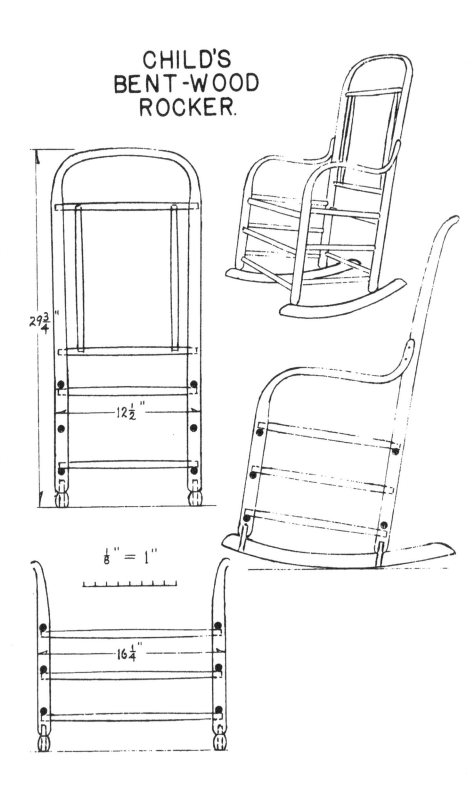

$29\frac{3}{4}$"

$12\frac{1}{2}$"

$\frac{1}{8}$" = 1"

$16\frac{1}{4}$"

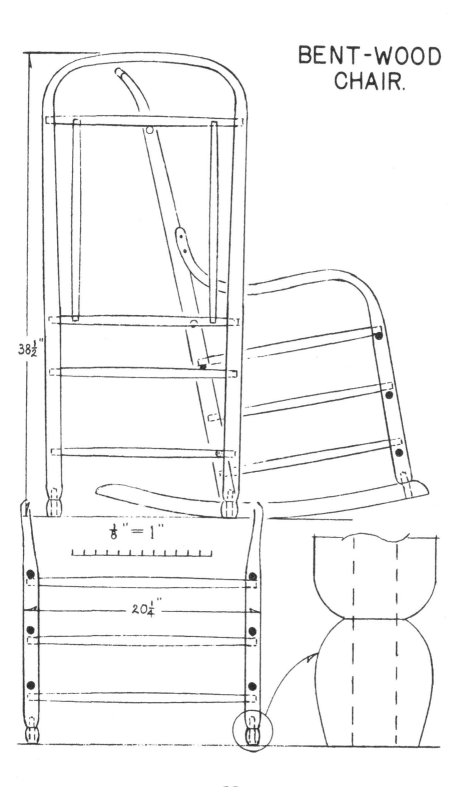

BENT-WOOD CHAIR.

$38\frac{1}{2}$"

$\frac{1}{8}$" = 1"

$20\frac{1}{4}$"

CHILD'S CHAIR.

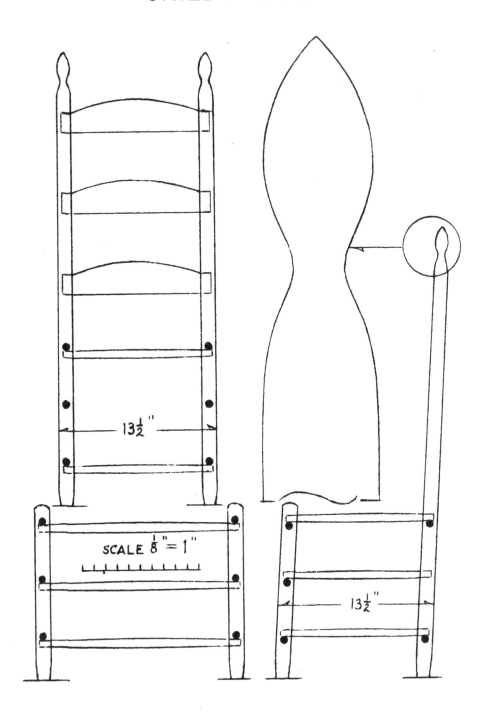

$13\frac{1}{2}''$

SCALE $\frac{1}{8}'' = 1''$

$13\frac{1}{2}''$

CHILD'S CHAIR.

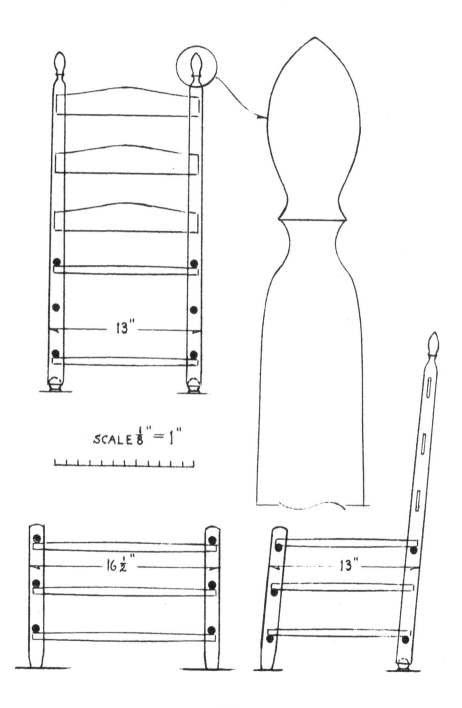

13"

SCALE $\frac{1}{8}$" = 1"

16$\frac{1}{2}$"

13"

35

TWO-SLAT
DINING CHAIR.

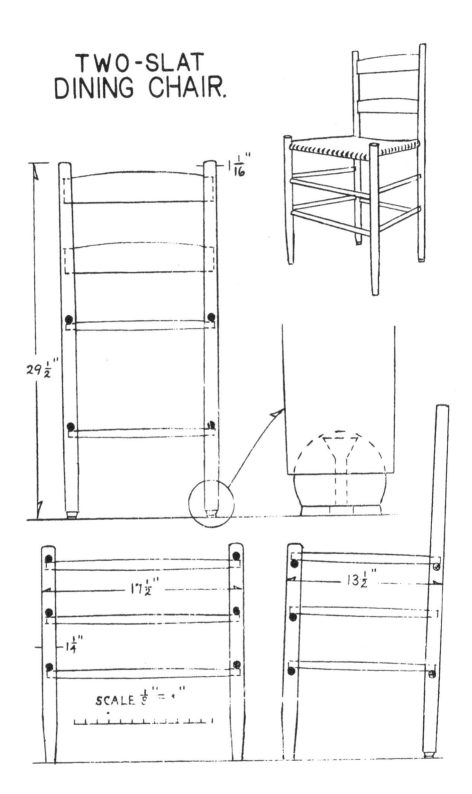

$1\frac{1}{16}''$

$29\frac{1}{2}''$

$17\frac{1}{2}''$

$1\frac{1}{4}''$

$13\frac{1}{2}''$

SCALE $\frac{1}{8}'' = 1''$

36

TWO-SLAT
DINING CHAIR

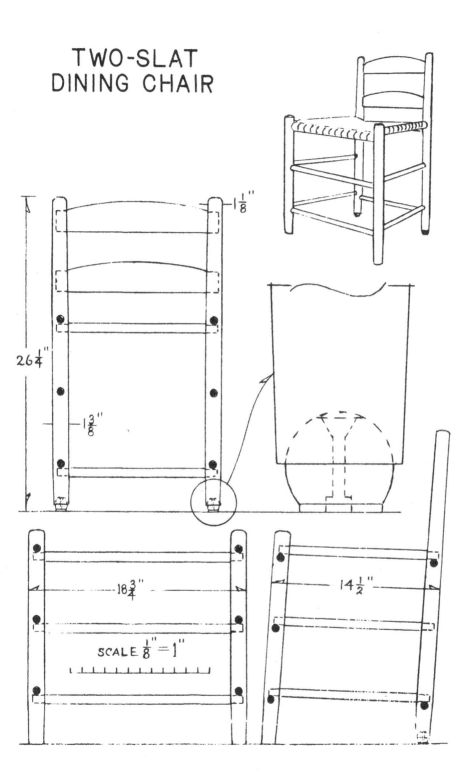

$1\frac{1}{8}''$

$26\frac{1}{4}''$

$1\frac{3}{8}''$

$18\frac{3}{4}''$

$14\frac{1}{2}''$

SCALE $\frac{1}{8}'' = 1''$

EARLY ROCKING CHAIR.

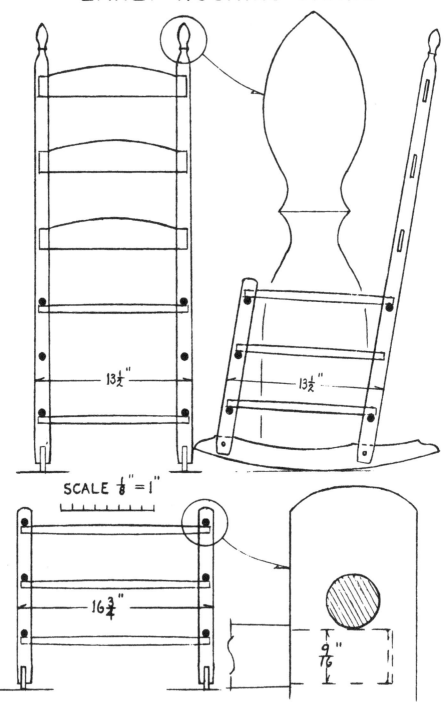

13½"

13½"

SCALE ⅛" = 1"

16¾"

9/16"

38

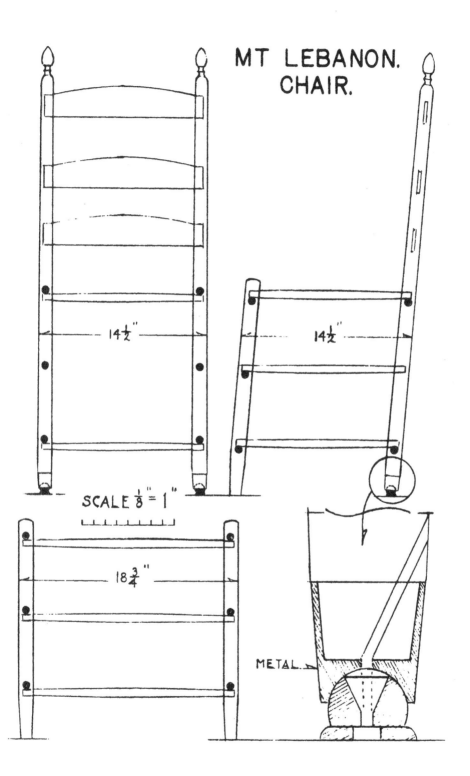

MT LEBANON.
CHAIR.

14½"

14½"

SCALE ⅛" = 1"

18¾"

METAL.

39

MT. LEBANON
ARMCHAIR.

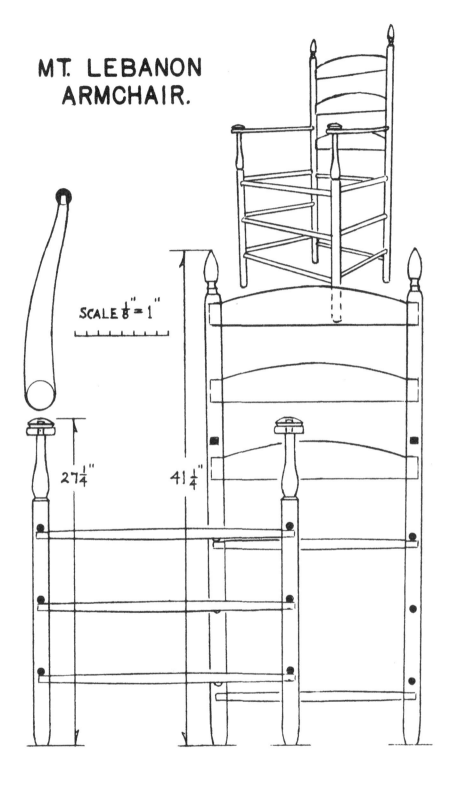

SCALE $\frac{1}{8}'' = 1''$

$27\frac{1}{4}''$

$41\frac{1}{4}''$

MT. LEBANON ARMCHAIR.

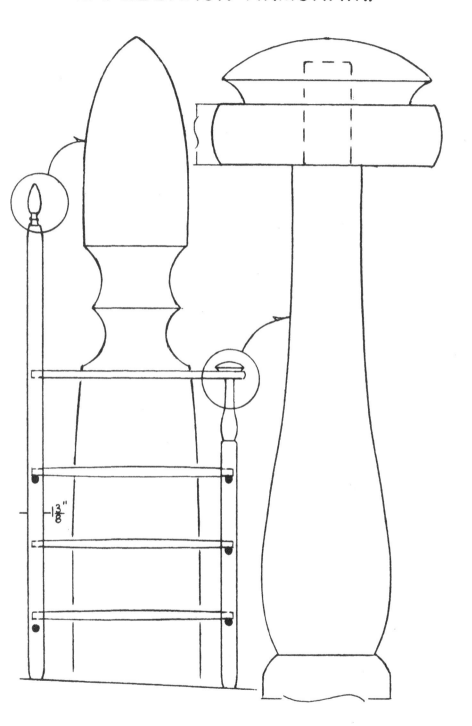

$1\frac{3}{8}''$

MT. LEBANON CHAIRS.

The following quotations and the descriptions
on the Plates are taken from a Shaker chair catalog
dated 1876.

" . . . a description and a representation of the
different sizes of chairs and foot benches which we
manufacture and sell. We would also call attention
of the public to the fact that there is no other
chair manufactory which is owned and operated by the
Shakers, except the one which is now in operation
and owned and operated by the Society of Shakers, at
Mount Lebanon, Columbia, county, N. Y. We deem it a
duty we owe the public to enlighten them in this
matter, owing to the fact that there are now several
manufacturers of chairs who have made and introduced
into market an imitation of our own styles of chairs,
which they sell for Shakers' Chairs, and which are
unquestionably bought by the public generally under
the impression that they are the real genuine article,
made by the Shakers at their establishment in Mount
Lebanon, N. Y. Of all the imitations of our chairs
which have come under our observation, there is none
which we would be willing to accept as our workmanship, nor would we be willing to stake our reputation
on their merits.

"The increasing demand for our chairs has prompted
us to increase the facilities for producing and
improving them. We have spared no expense or labor
in our endeavors to produce an article that cannot
be surpassed in any respect, and which combines all
the advantages of durability, simplicity and lightness.

"The bars across the top of back posts are intend-
ed for cushions, but will be furnished to order without additional cost.

"Many of our friends who see the Shakers' chairs for the first time may be led to suppose that the chair business is a new thing for the Shakers to engage in. This is not the fact, however, and may surprise even some of the oldest manufacturers to learn that the Shakers were pioneers in the business after the establishment of the independence of the country.

"The principles as well as the rules of the Society forbid the trustees or any of their assistants doing business on the credit system, either in the purchase or sale of merchandise, or making bargains or contracts. This we consider good policy, and a safe way of doing business, checking speculative or dishonest propensities, and averting financial panics and disasters. We sell with the understanding that all bills are to be cash.

"Look for our trade-mark before purchasing - no chair is genuine without it. Our trade-mark is a gold transfer, and is designed to be ornamental; but, if objectionable to purchasers, it can be easily removed without defacing the furniture in the least, by wetting a sponge or piece of cotton cloth with AQUA AMMONIA, and rubbing it until it is loosened."

The Shakers' Slat Back Chairs, with Rockers.

WORSTED LACE SEATS.

Showing a Comparison of Sizes.

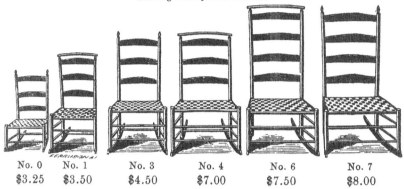

No. 0	No. 1	No. 3	No. 4	No. 6	No. 7
$3.25	$3.50	$4.50	$7.00	$7.50	$8.00

The Shakers' Web Back Chairs, With Rockers.

WORSTED LACE SEATS AND BACKS.

Showing a Comparison of Sizes.

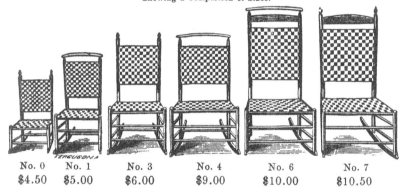

No. 0	No. 1	No. 3	No. 4	No. 6	No. 7
$4.50	$5.00	$6.00	$9.00	$10.00	$10.50

THE SHAKERS' UPHOLSTERED CHAIRS.

WITHOUT ARMS.

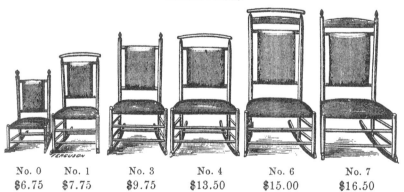

No. 0	No. 1	No. 3	No. 4	No. 6	No. 7
$6.75	$7.75	$9.75	$13.50	$15.00	$16.50

44

The Shakers' Slat Back Chairs, with Arms and Rockers.

WORSTED LACE SEATS.

Showing a Comparison of Sizes.

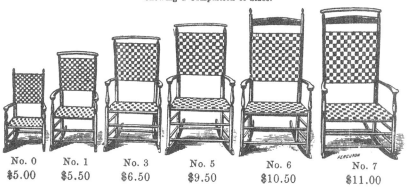

No. 0	No. 1	No. 3	No. 5	No. 6	No. 7
$3.50	$4.00	$5.00	$7.00	$8.00	$8.50

The Shakers' Web Back Chairs, with Arms and Rockers.

WORSTED LACE SEATS AND BACKS.

Showing a Comparison of Sizes.

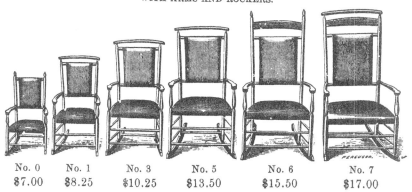

No. 0	No. 1	No. 3	No. 5	No. 6	No. 7
$5.00	$5.50	$6.50	$9.50	$10.50	$11.00

THE SHAKERS' UPHOLSTERED CHAIRS.

WITH ARMS AND ROCKERS.

No. 0	No. 1	No. 3	No. 5	No. 6	No. 7
$7.00	$8.25	$10.25	$13.50	$15.50	$17.00

MT. LEBANON CHAIR NO. 7.

"This is our largest chair, and on the top of the back posts is a bar which we attach to all the chairs which are designed for cushions.

"We have this chair with or without rockers or arms.

"Remember that all chairs are imitations which are not made and sold by the Society of Shakers, Mount Lebanon, N. Y. Don't let any outside party sell you the imitation or spurious chairs which may bear the name of Shaker chair."

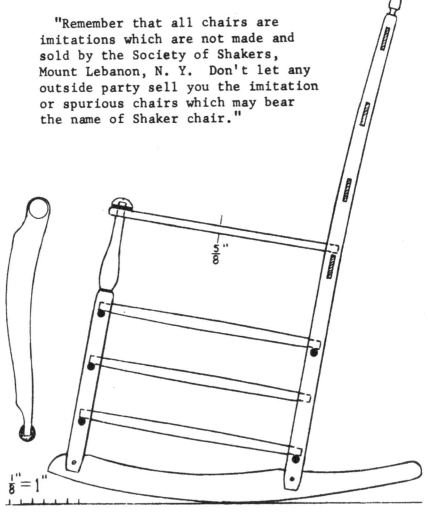

$\frac{5}{8}$"

$\frac{1}{8}" = 1"$

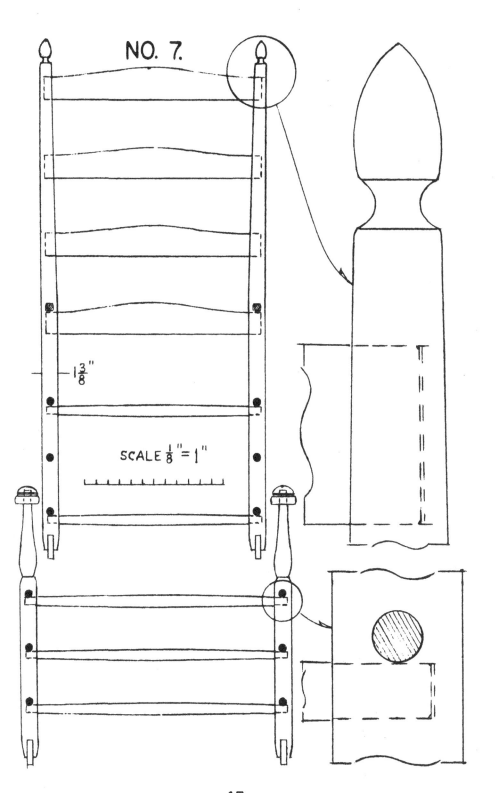

NO. 7.

$1\frac{3}{8}''$

SCALE $\frac{1}{8}'' = 1''$

47

MT. LEBANON CHAIR NO. 6.

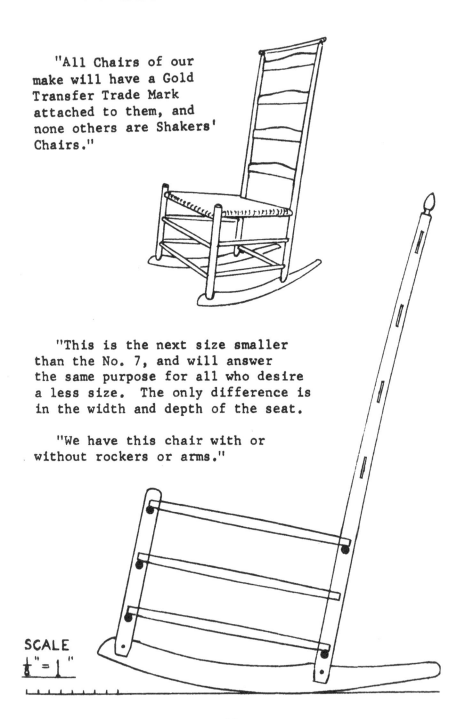

"All Chairs of our
make will have a Gold
Transfer Trade Mark
attached to them, and
none others are Shakers'
Chairs."

"This is the next size smaller
than the No. 7, and will answer
the same purpose for all who desire
a less size. The only difference is
in the width and depth of the seat.

"We have this chair with or
without rockers or arms."

SCALE
$\frac{1}{8}$" = 1"

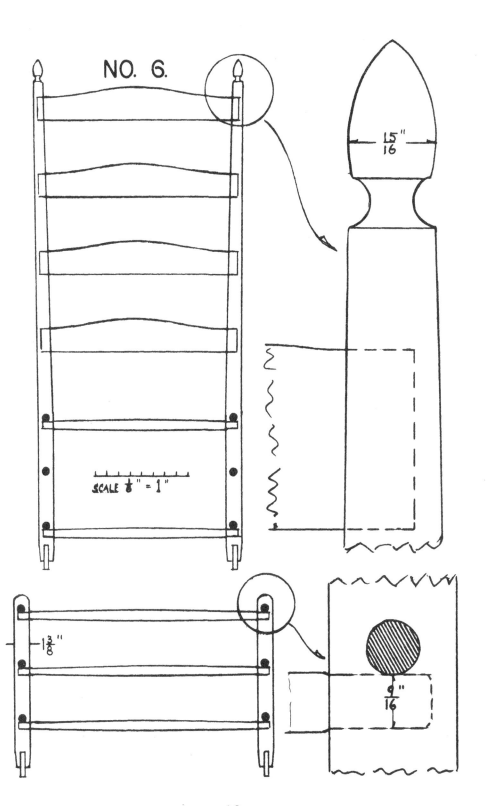

NO. 6.

SCALE $\frac{1}{8}$" = 1"

$\frac{15}{16}$"

$1\frac{3}{8}$"

$\frac{9}{16}$"

MT. LEBANON CHAIR NO. 5.

"This size is well adapted for dining or office use, when an arm chair is desirable. We have a smaller size, with only two back slats and plain top posts, for table use, and without arms.

"We do not have this chair without the arms.

"The Shakers do not make or sell any of the cheap quality of chairs, but we claim for every one of them the same quality and price invariably."

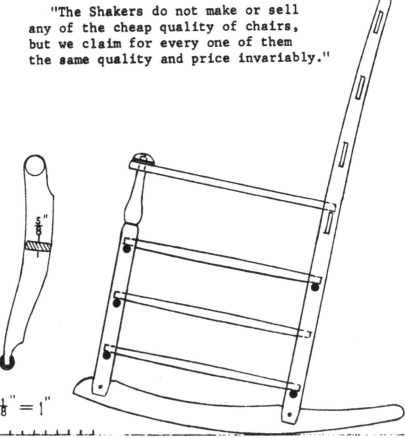

$\frac{1}{8}" = 1"$

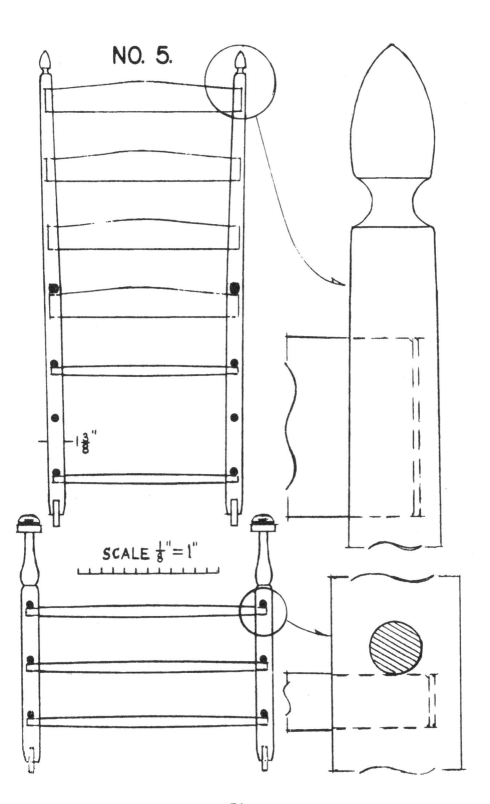

NO. 5.

$1\frac{3}{8}''$

SCALE $\frac{1}{8}''=1''$

51

MT. LEBANON CHAIR NO. 4.

"This chair is a great favorite
with the ladies. It is broad on
the seat, and very easy. We do
not make this size with arms, and
the back is lower than the large
arm chairs, but have them with or
without rockers."

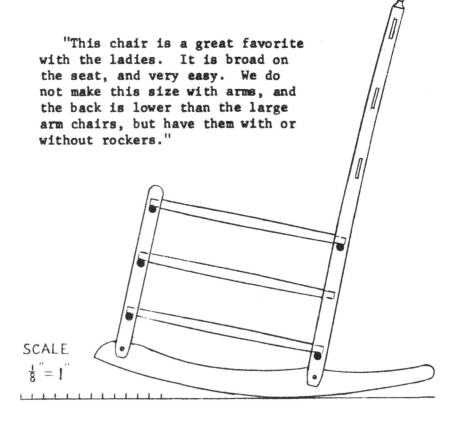

SCALE

$\frac{1}{8}" = 1"$

MT. LEBANON CHAIR NO. 4.

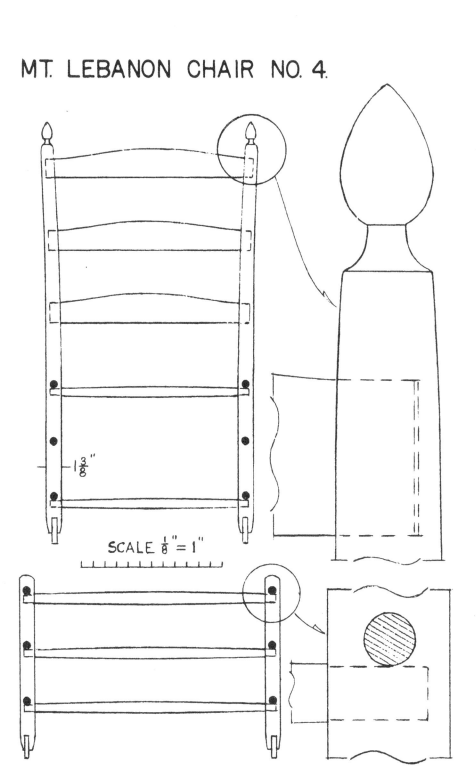

SCALE $\frac{1}{8}"= 1"$

$1\frac{3}{8}"$

53

MT. LEBANON CHAIR NO. 3.

"This is a favorite
sewing chair, and for all
general purposes about
the chamber and sitting
room. We have this size
with arms, rockers, or
without either."

"Those who want a very comfortable
chair, and do not want to expend enough
for a cushioned chair, would do well
to get one with a web back. It is both
comfortable and neat, and requires only
a trifling additional cost more than
the slat backs."

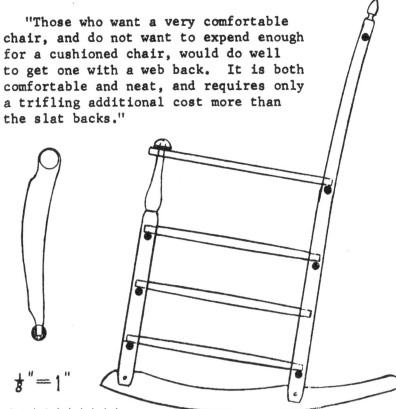

$\frac{1}{8}'' = 1''$

MT. LEBANON CHAIR NO. 3.

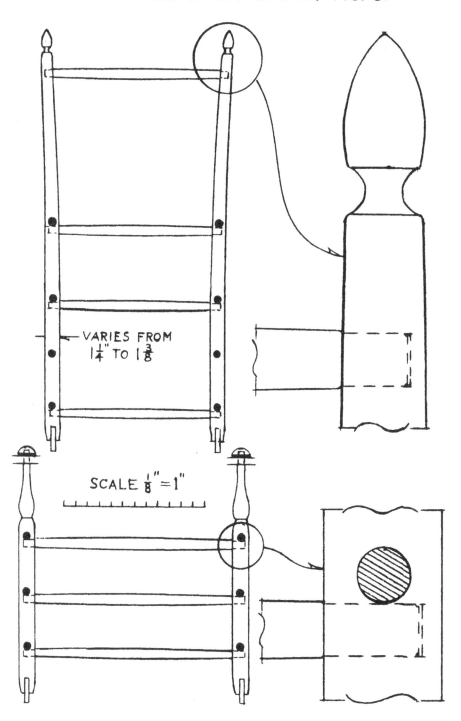

VARIES FROM
$1\frac{1}{4}"$ TO $1\frac{3}{8}$

SCALE $\frac{1}{8}" = 1"$

MT. LEBANON CHAIR NO. I.

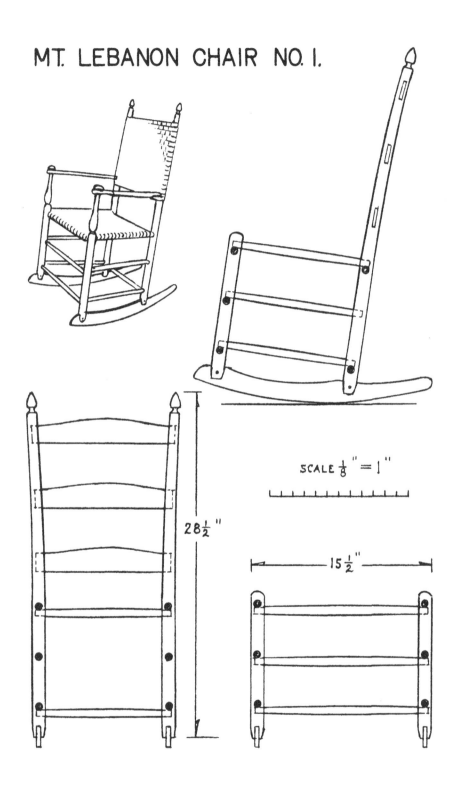

SCALE $\frac{1}{8}$ " = 1 "

$28\frac{1}{2}$ "

$15\frac{1}{2}$ "

MT. LEBANON CHAIR NO. I.

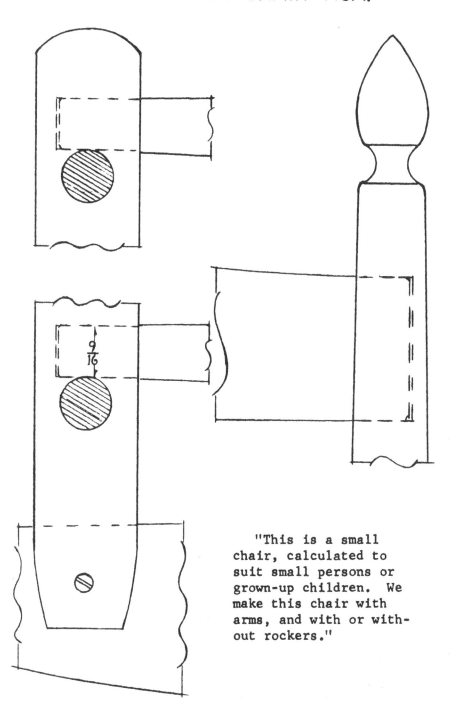

"This is a small chair, calculated to suit small persons or grown-up children. We make this chair with arms, and with or without rockers."

MT. LEBANON CHAIR NO. O.

SCALE ⅛" = 1"

MT. LEBANON CHAIR NO. O.

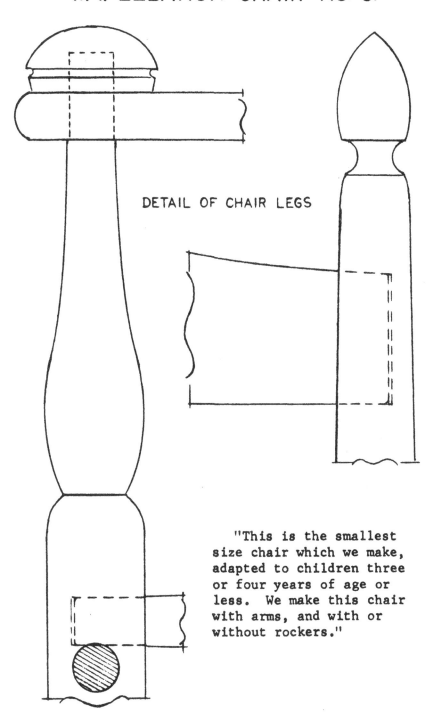

DETAIL OF CHAIR LEGS

"This is the smallest
size chair which we make,
adapted to children three
or four years of age or
less. We make this chair
with arms, and with or
without rockers."

CHAIR FINIALS.

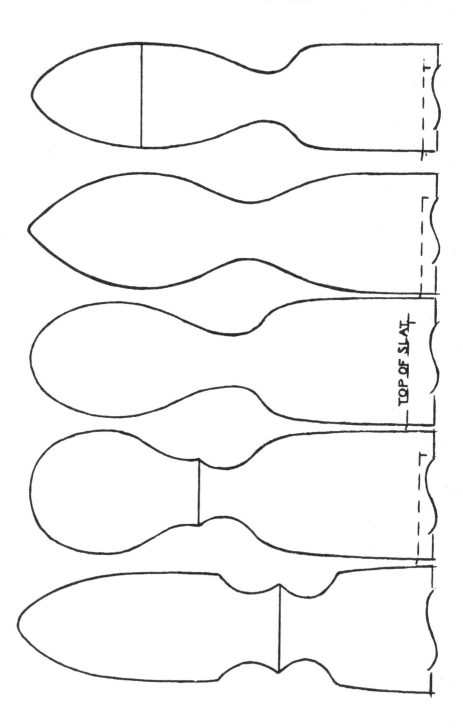

CHAIR FINIALS.

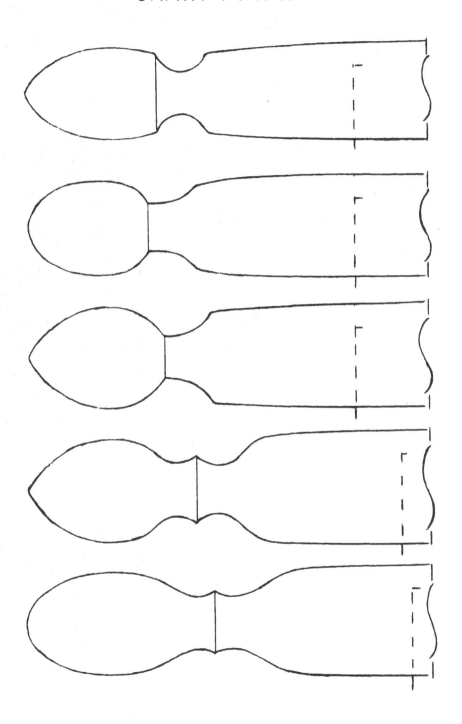

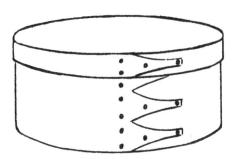

OVAL BOX.

INSIDE MEAS. OF BOX $7\frac{1}{2}'' \times 10\frac{7}{8}''$

COVER TO FIT

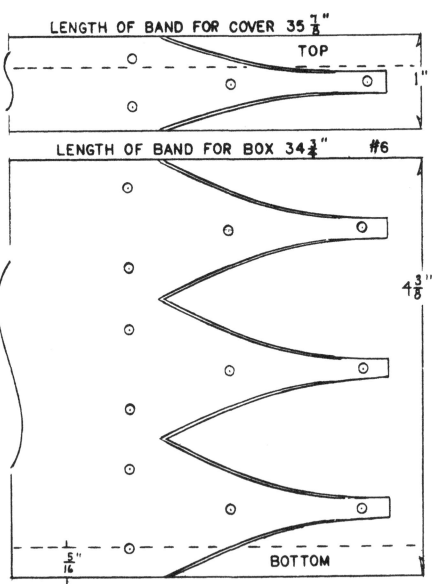

LENGTH OF BAND FOR COVER $35\frac{7}{8}''$

TOP

$1''$

LENGTH OF BAND FOR BOX $34\frac{3}{4}''$　　#6

$4\frac{3}{8}''$

$\frac{5}{16}''$

BOTTOM

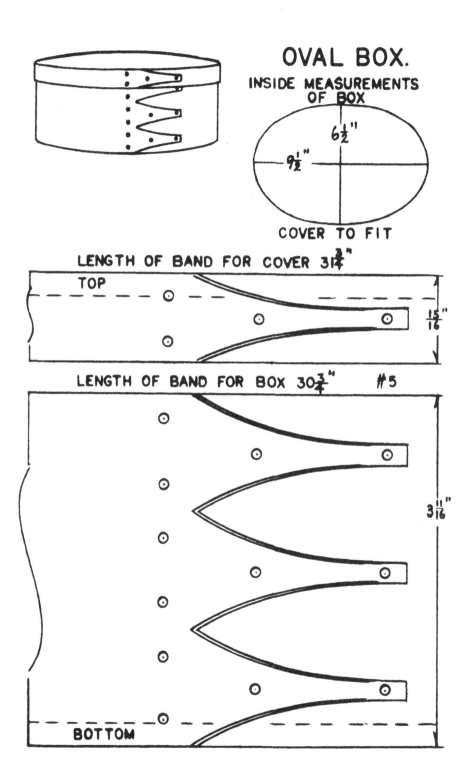

OVAL BOX.

INSIDE MEASUREMENTS OF BOX

$6\frac{1}{2}$"

$9\frac{1}{2}$"

COVER TO FIT

LENGTH OF BAND FOR COVER $31\frac{3}{4}$"

TOP

$\frac{15}{16}$"

LENGTH OF BAND FOR BOX $30\frac{3}{4}$"   #5

$3\frac{11}{16}$"

BOTTOM

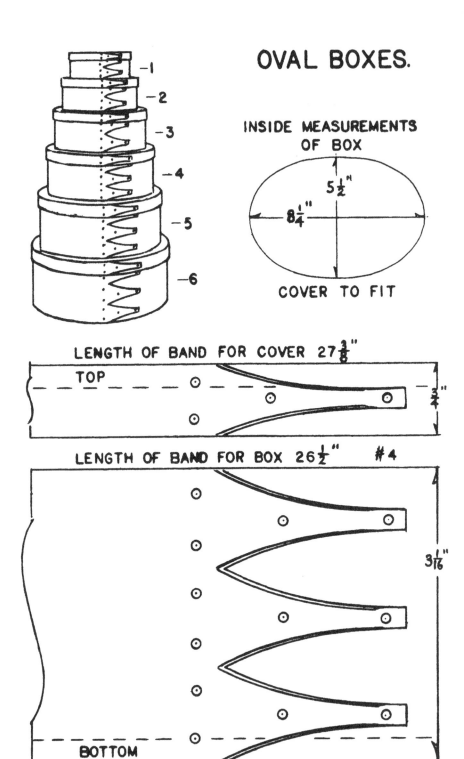

OVAL BOXES.

INSIDE MEASUREMENTS
OF BOX

$5\frac{1}{2}"$

$8\frac{1}{4}"$

COVER TO FIT

LENGTH OF BAND FOR COVER $27\frac{3}{8}"$

TOP

$\frac{3}{4}"$

LENGTH OF BAND FOR BOX $26\frac{1}{2}"$ #4

$3\frac{1}{16}"$

BOTTOM

OVAL BOXES.

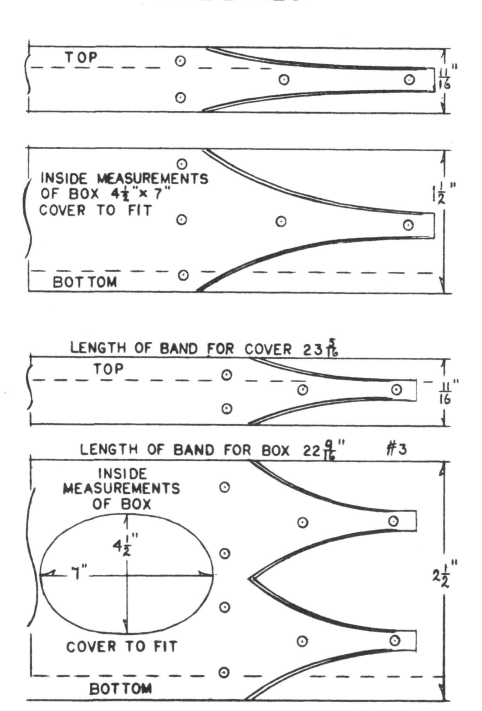

TOP

INSIDE MEASUREMENTS
OF BOX 4½"× 7"
COVER TO FIT

BOTTOM

$\frac{11}{16}$"

$1\frac{1}{2}$"

LENGTH OF BAND FOR COVER 23$\frac{5}{16}$

TOP

$\frac{11}{16}$"

LENGTH OF BAND FOR BOX 22$\frac{9}{16}$"   #3

INSIDE
MEASUREMENTS
OF BOX

4½"

7"

COVER TO FIT

BOTTOM

$2\frac{1}{2}$"

OVAL BOXES.

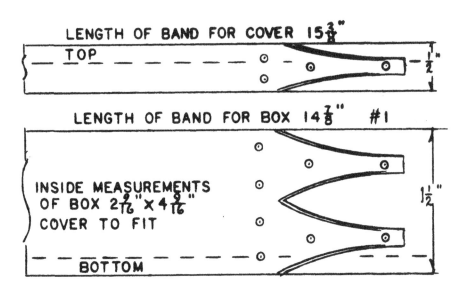

LENGTH OF BAND FOR COVER 15¾"

TOP

½"

LENGTH OF BAND FOR BOX 14⅞"   #1

INSIDE MEASUREMENTS
OF BOX 2 9/16" X 4 9/16"
COVER TO FIT

BOTTOM

1½"

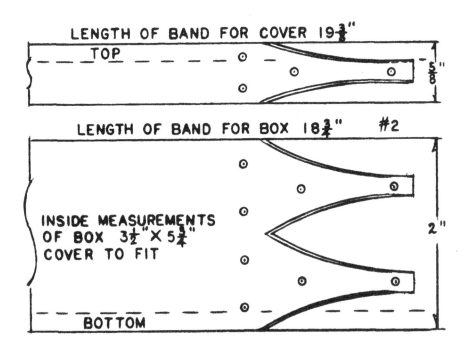

LENGTH OF BAND FOR COVER 19¾"

TOP

⅝"

LENGTH OF BAND FOR BOX 18¾"   #2

INSIDE MEASUREMENTS
OF BOX 3½" X 5¾"
COVER TO FIT

BOTTOM

2"

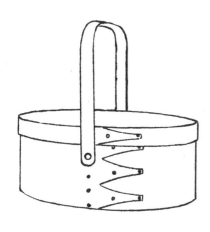

SEWING BOX.

INSIDE MEASUREMENTS OF BOX

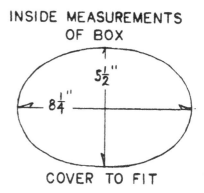

$5\frac{1}{2}''$

$8\frac{1}{4}''$

COVER TO FIT

LENGTH OF BAND FOR COVER $27\frac{3}{8}''$

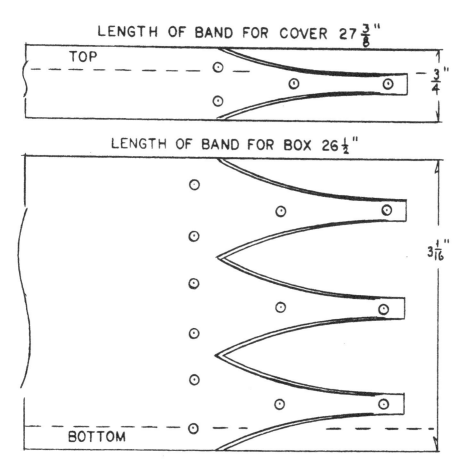

TOP

$\frac{3}{4}''$

LENGTH OF BAND FOR BOX $26\frac{1}{2}''$

$3\frac{1}{16}''$

BOTTOM

CARRIER.

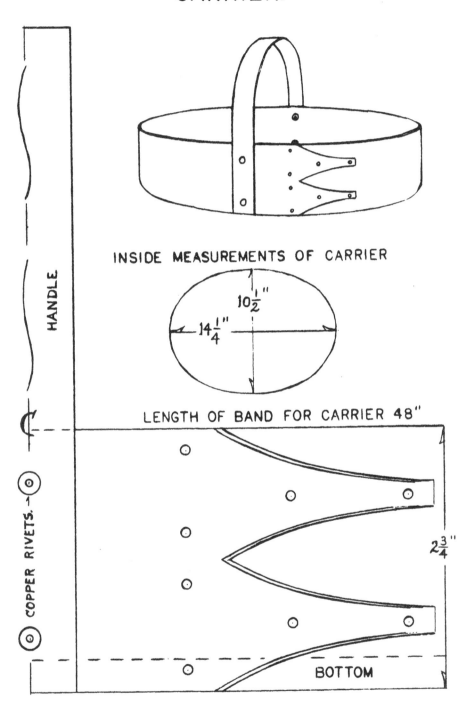

INSIDE MEASUREMENTS OF CARRIER

$10\frac{1}{2}''$

$14\frac{1}{4}''$

LENGTH OF BAND FOR CARRIER 48"

HANDLE

COPPER RIVETS.

$2\frac{3}{4}''$

BOTTOM

CARRIERS.

INSIDE MEAS.
OF CARRIERS
$10\frac{3}{8}$" × $14\frac{1}{2}$"

HEIGHT TO TOP
OF HANDLE
$9\frac{3}{4}$"

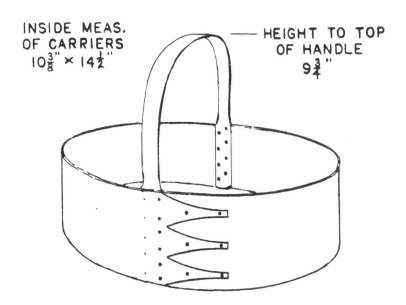

LENGTH OF BAND
FOR CARRIERS
52"

HEIGHT TO TOP
OF HANDLE
$11\frac{1}{4}$"

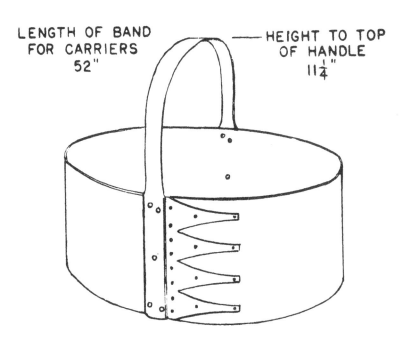

SPITTOON OR "SPIT-BOX"

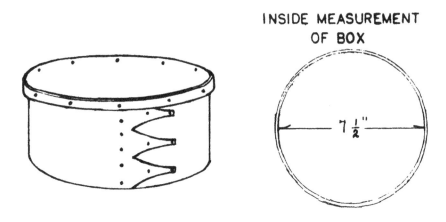

INSIDE MEASUREMENT
OF BOX

$7\frac{1}{2}"$

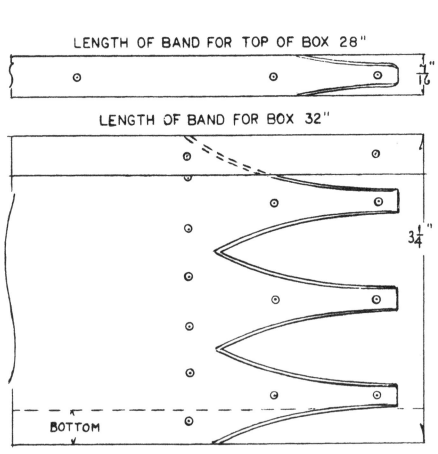

LENGTH OF BAND FOR TOP OF BOX 28"

$\frac{1}{16}"$

LENGTH OF BAND FOR BOX 32"

$3\frac{1}{4}"$

BOTTOM

PINE TRAY 9" × 15"

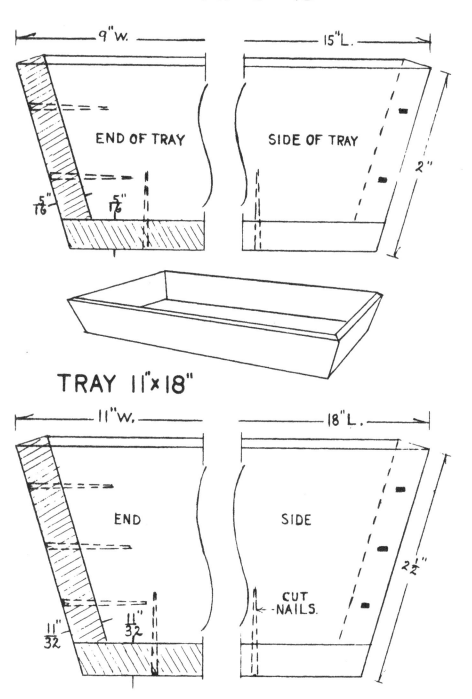

9" W.

END OF TRAY

SIDE OF TRAY

15" L.

2"

$\frac{5}{16}$"

$\frac{5}{16}$"

TRAY 11" × 18"

11" W.

END

SIDE

18" L.

2$\frac{1}{2}$"

$\frac{11}{32}$"

$\frac{11}{32}$"

CUT
NAILS.

DINING ROOM TRAY.

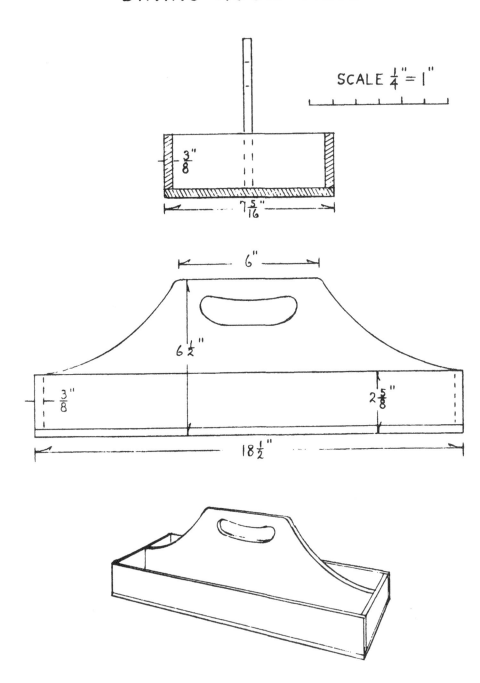

SCALE $\frac{1}{4}" = 1"$

$\frac{3}{8}"$

$7\frac{5}{16}"$

$6"$

$6\frac{1}{2}"$

$\frac{3}{8}"$

$2\frac{5}{8}"$

$18\frac{1}{2}"$

PINE DINING ROOM TRAY.

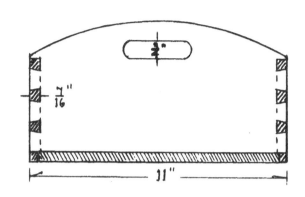

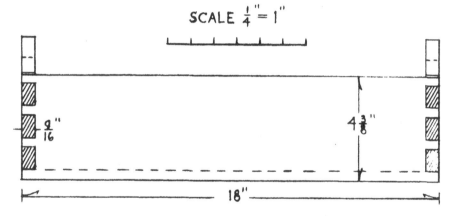

SCALE $\frac{1}{4}'' = 1''$

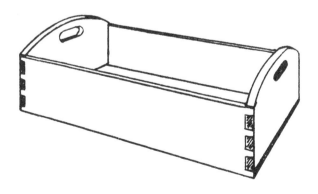

73

CLAMP-ON CUSHIONS.

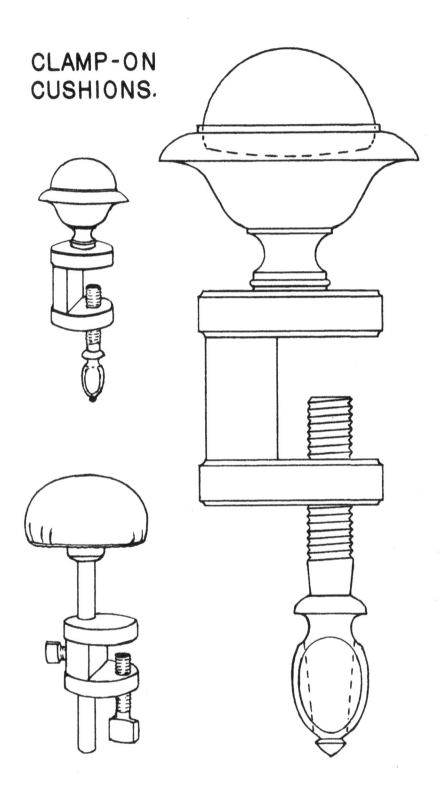

SPOOL HOLDER.

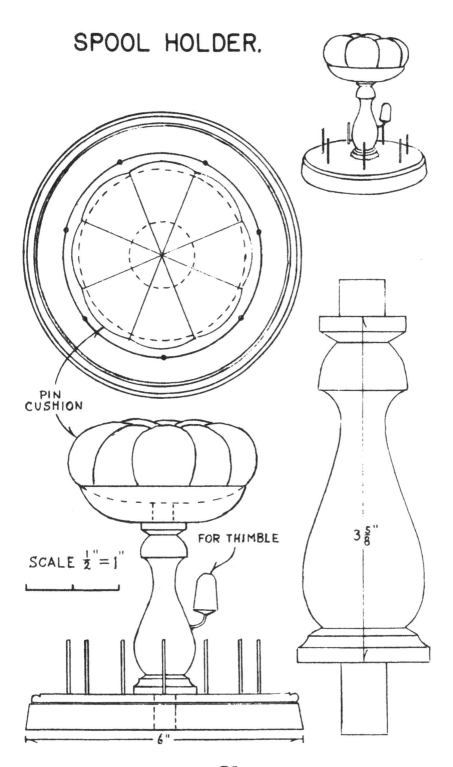

PIN
CUSHION

FOR THIMBLE

SCALE $\frac{1}{2}" = 1"$

$3\frac{5}{8}"$

6"

DIPPER.

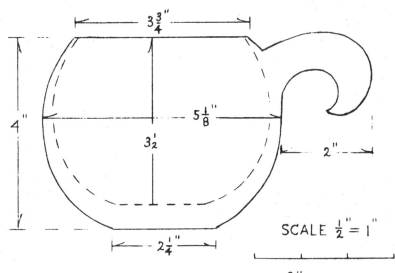

3 ¾"

4"

3 ½'

5 ⅛"

2"

2 ¼"

SCALE ½" = 1"

BERRY BOX.

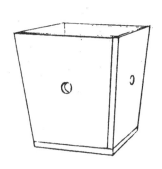

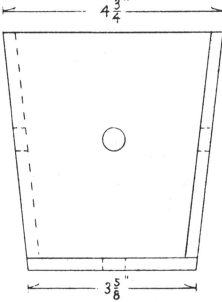

4 ¾"

3 ⅝"

DIPPER.

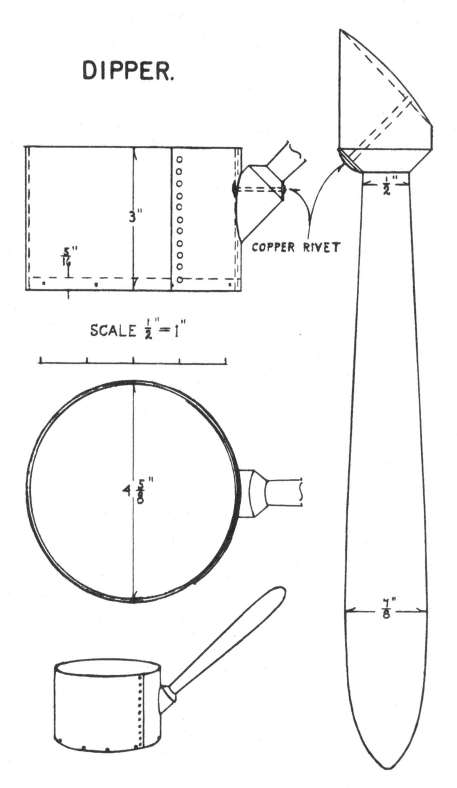

3"

$\frac{5}{16}$"

COPPER RIVET

SCALE $\frac{1}{2}$" = 1"

$4\frac{5}{8}$"

$\frac{1}{2}$"

$\frac{7}{8}$"

CANDLE SCONCE.
PINE.

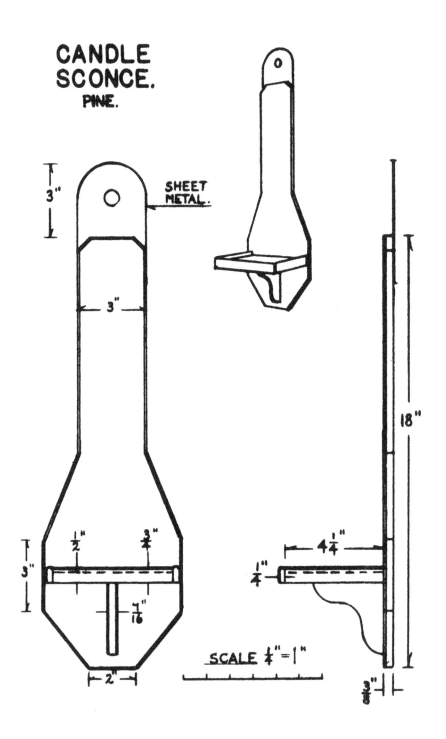

SHEET METAL.

3"

3"

3"

½"

¾"

3"

7/16"

2"

18"

4¼"

¼"

3/4"

SCALE ¼"=1"

78

CANDLE SCONCE.

PINE.

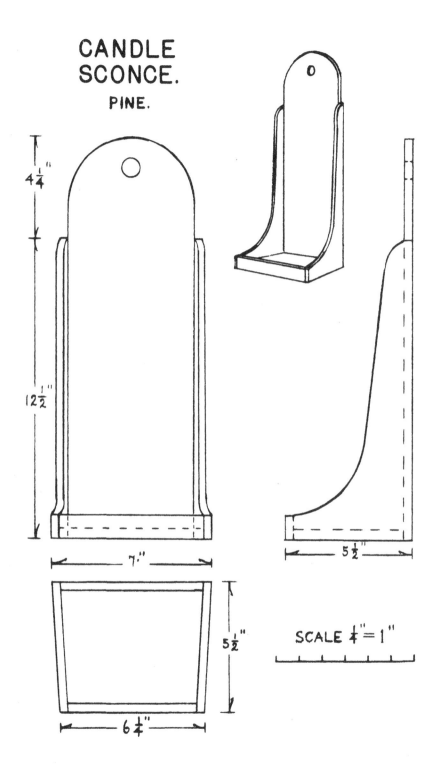

$4\frac{1}{4}$"

$12\frac{1}{2}$"

7."

$5\frac{1}{2}$"

$5\frac{1}{2}$"

$6\frac{1}{4}$"

SCALE $\frac{1}{4}$"$=1$"

CANDLESTAND.

CHERRY

SCALE $\frac{1}{4}'' = 1''$

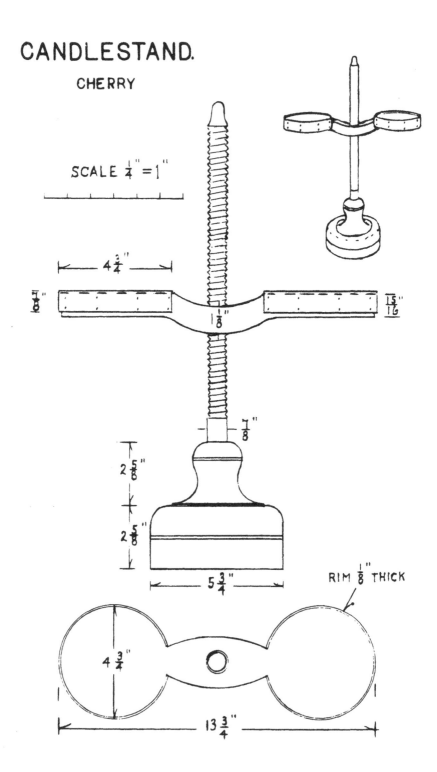

4 $\frac{3}{4}''$

$\frac{7}{8}''$

$1\frac{1}{8}''$

$\frac{15}{16}''$

$\frac{1}{8}''$

2 $\frac{5}{8}''$

2 $\frac{5}{8}''$

5 $\frac{3}{4}''$

RIM $\frac{1}{8}''$ THICK

4 $\frac{3}{4}''$

13 $\frac{3}{4}''$

COAT HANGERS.

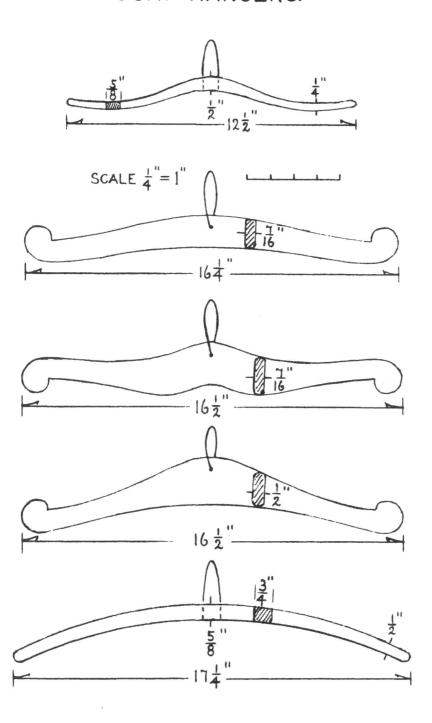

SCALE $\frac{1}{4}$" = 1"

INDEX

Asterisks after plate numbers refer to drawings made from pieces in the collection of Dr. and Mrs. Edward D. Andrews.

Shop Drawings of Shaker Furniture and Woodenware

Volume 2

Measured Drawings
by Ejner Handberg

ACKNOWLEDGMENTS

This second book of *Shop Drawings of Shaker Furniture and Woodenware* includes pieces which have been in my shop, as well as several other interesting pieces from collections mentioned below.

Special thanks are due to Mrs. Edward Deming Andrews for permission to make measured drawings of several more pieces from the Andrews collection and for the help and information given me.

I am also very grateful for cooperation and for similar help and permission at Hancock Shaker Village, Hancock, Massachusetts and the Shaker Museum, Old Chatham, New York.

Although the Shaker cabinetmakers were obliged to make their furniture and woodenware with utility in mind, their work is eagerly sought today by museums and private collectors for its simplicity and beauty. I wish to thank several of these collectors for allowing me to examine and make drawings of Shaker pieces in their possession.

E.H.
1975

CONTENTS

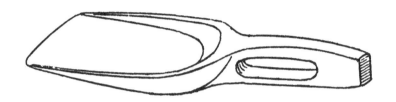

"BEAUTY RESTS ON UTILITY"

WALL CLOCK
BY I. N. YOUNGS
HANCOCK SHAKER VILLAGE, HANCOCK MASS.

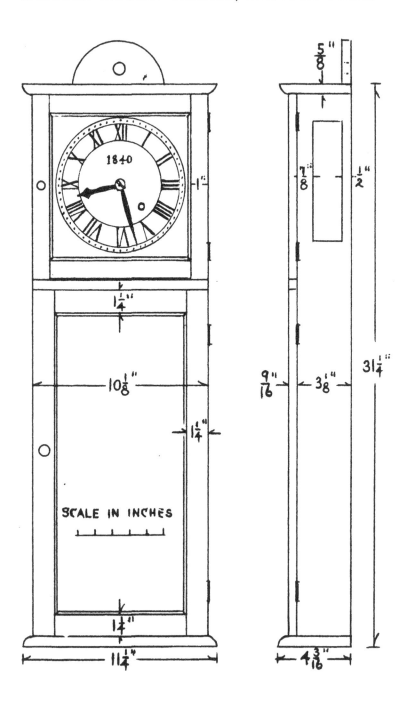

SCALE IN INCHES

2

WALL CLOCK
BY I. N. YOUNGS
HANCOCK SHAKER VILLAGE, HANCOCK MASS.

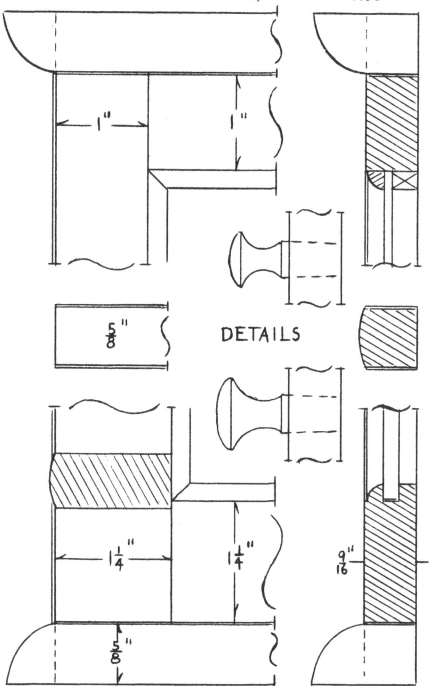

DETAILS

DESK
CHERRY

FROM ANDREWS
COLLECTION

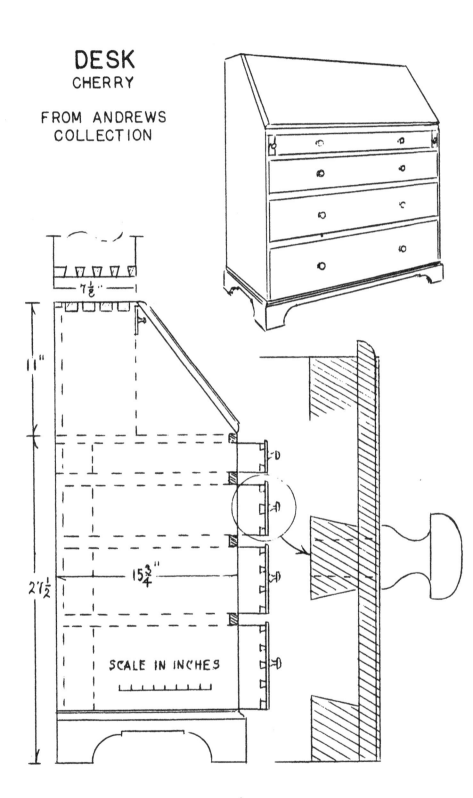

$7\frac{1}{8}$"

11"

$15\frac{3}{4}$"

$2'7\frac{1}{2}$

SCALE IN INCHES

4

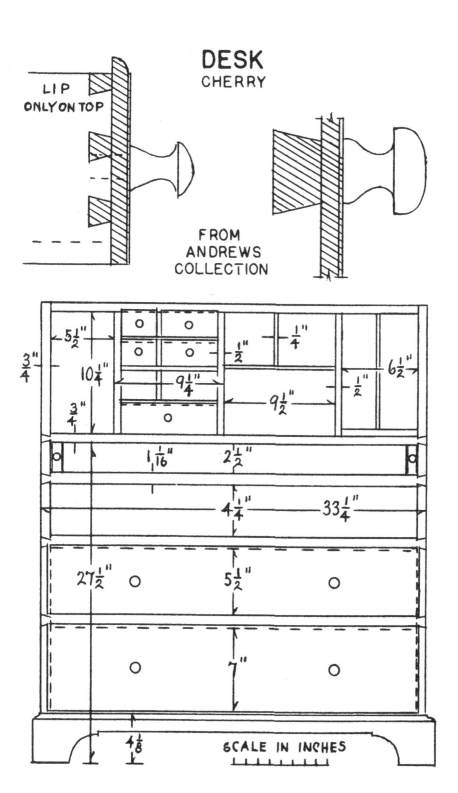

DESK
CHERRY

LIP ONLY ON TOP

FROM ANDREWS COLLECTION

SCALE IN INCHES

5

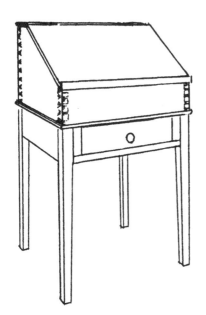

PINE DESK

THE SHAKER MUSEUM,
OLD CHATHAM, N.Y.

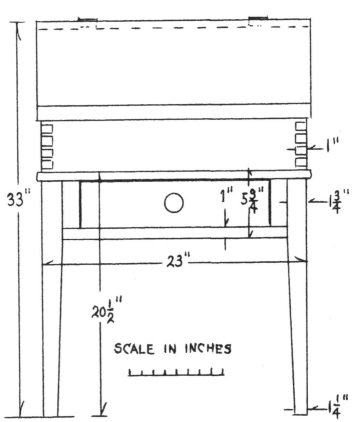

33"

1"

1" 5¾"

1¾"

23"

20½"

SCALE IN INCHES

1¼"

6

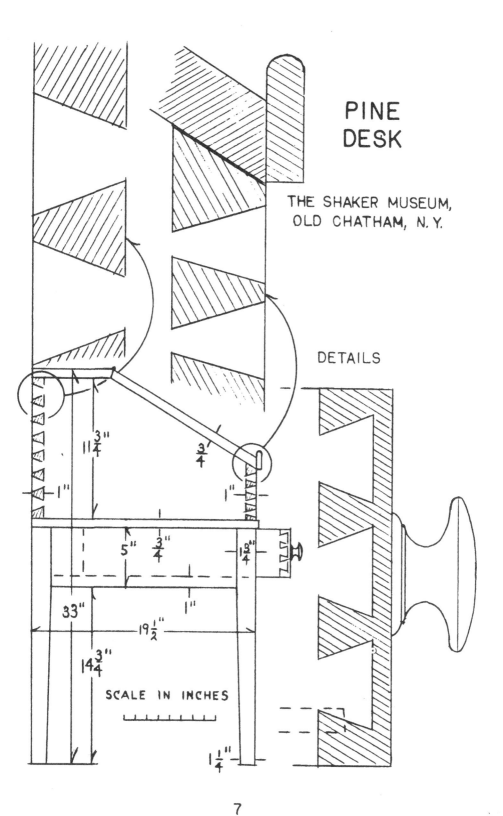

PINE DESK

THE SHAKER MUSEUM,
OLD CHATHAM, N.Y.

DETAILS

$11\frac{3}{4}$"

$\frac{3}{4}$'

1"

1"

5" $\frac{3}{4}$"

$1\frac{3}{4}$"

33"

1"

$19\frac{1}{2}$"

$14\frac{3}{4}$"

SCALE IN INCHES

$1\frac{1}{4}$"

7

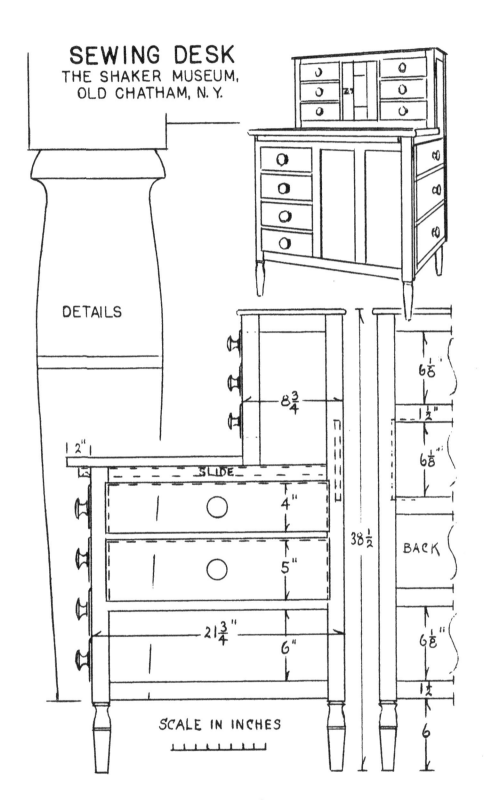

SEWING DESK
THE SHAKER MUSEUM,
OLD CHATHAM, N.Y.

DETAILS

SLIDE

2"

$8\frac{3}{4}$

4"

5"

$21\frac{3}{4}$"

6"

$38\frac{1}{2}$

$6\frac{1}{8}$

$1\frac{1}{2}$"

$6\frac{1}{8}$"

BACK

$6\frac{1}{8}$"

$1\frac{1}{2}$

6

SCALE IN INCHES

8

SEWING DESK
THE SHAKER MUSEUM, OLD CHATHAM, N.Y.

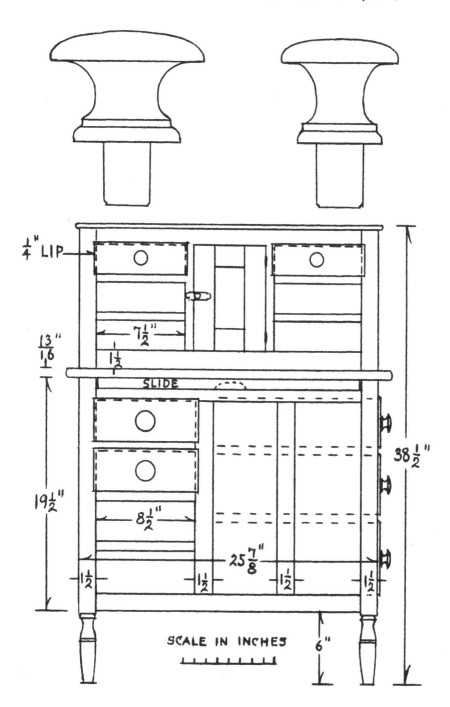

$\frac{1}{4}$" LIP

$\frac{13}{16}$"

$7\frac{1}{2}$"

$1\frac{1}{2}$

SLIDE

$19\frac{1}{2}$"

$8\frac{1}{2}$"

$38\frac{1}{2}$"

$25\frac{7}{8}$"

$1\frac{1}{2}$

$1\frac{1}{2}$

$1\frac{1}{2}$

$1\frac{1}{2}$

SCALE IN INCHES

6"

PINE
SEWING DESK

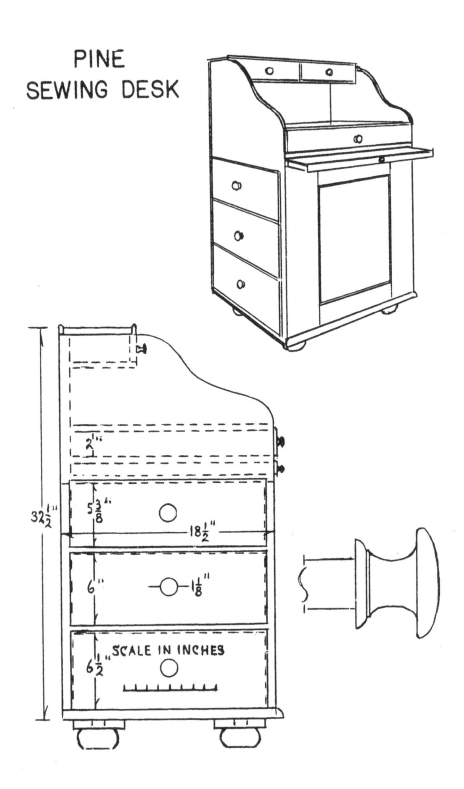

SCALE IN INCHES

10

PINE SEWING DESK

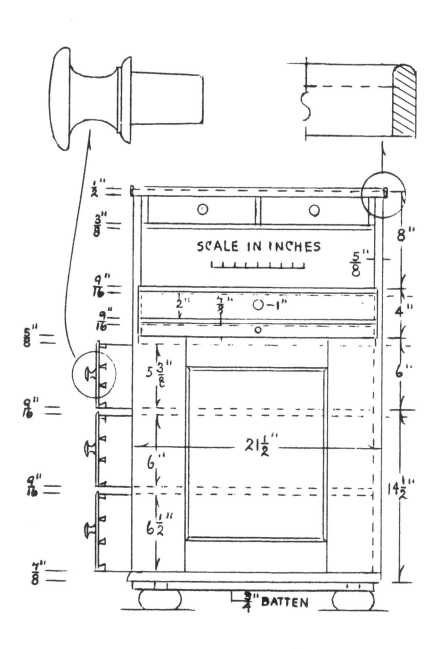

SCALE IN INCHES

$\frac{3}{4}$" BATTEN

SEWING TABLE
THE SHAKER MUSEUM, OLD CHATHAM, N.Y.
CHERRY WITH PINE TOP

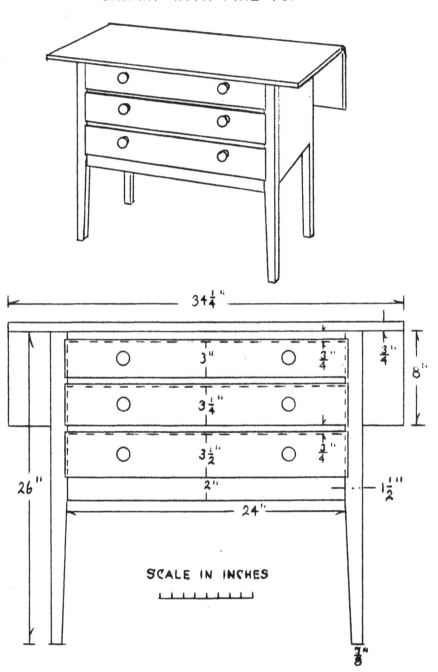

SCALE IN INCHES

SEWING TABLE
THE SHAKER MUSEUM, OLD CHATHAM, N. Y.

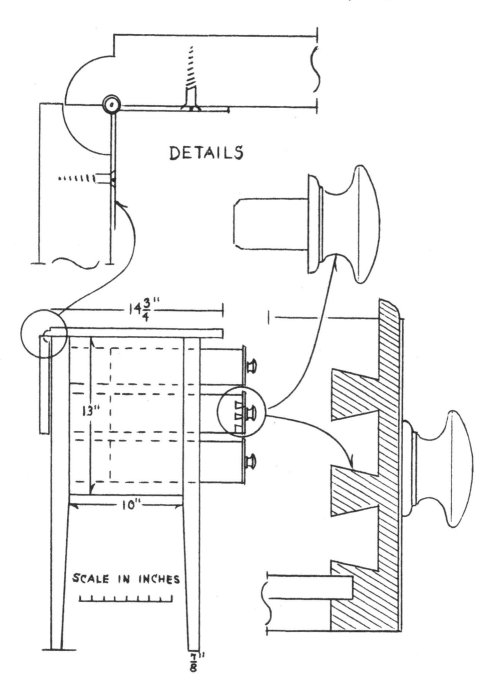

DETAILS

$14\frac{3}{4}$"

13"

10"

SCALE IN INCHES

$\frac{7}{8}$"

PINE TABLE
STAINED RED
FROM ANDREWS COLLECTION

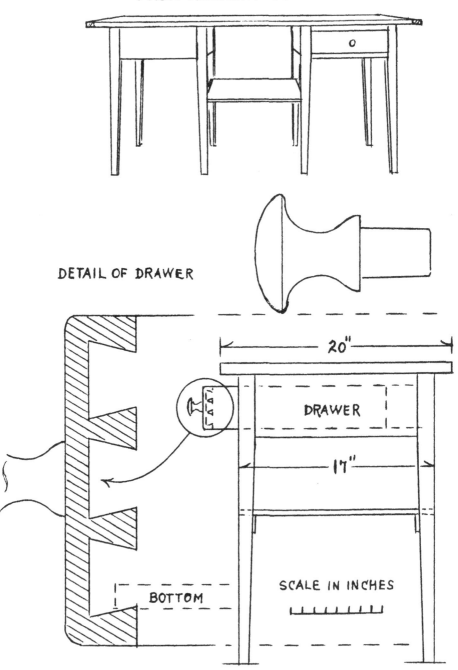

DETAIL OF DRAWER

20"

DRAWER

17"

BOTTOM

SCALE IN INCHES

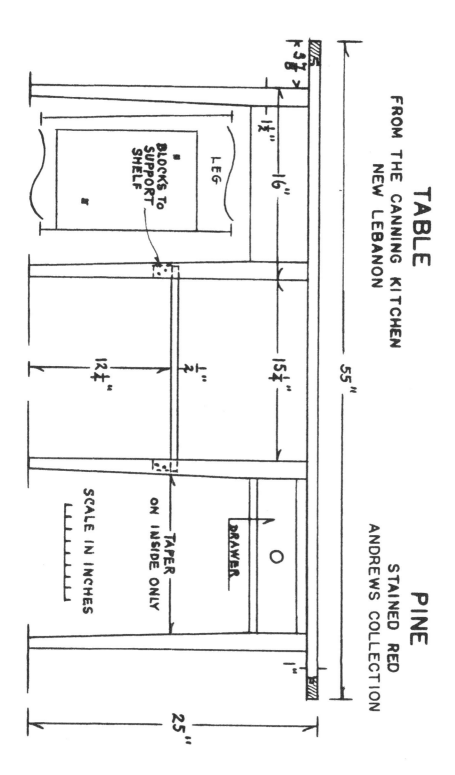

TABLE

FROM THE CANNING KITCHEN
NEW LEBANON

PINE
STAINED RED
ANDREWS COLLECTION

55"

25"

16"

15¼"

1¾"

3⅞

LEG

BLOCKS TO
SUPPORT
SHELF

12¼"

½"

TAPER
ON INSIDE ONLY

DRAWER

1"

SCALE IN INCHES

BAKE-ROOM TABLE
FROM ANDREWS COLLECTION

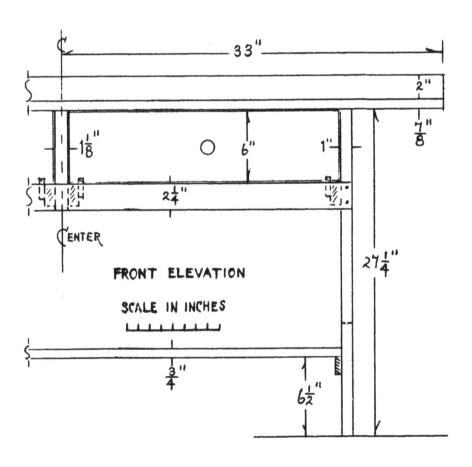

33"

2"

7/8"

1⅛"

6"

1"

2¼"

CENTER

FRONT ELEVATION

SCALE IN INCHES

27¼"

¾"

6½"

BAKE-ROOM TABLE
FROM ANDREWS COLLECTION

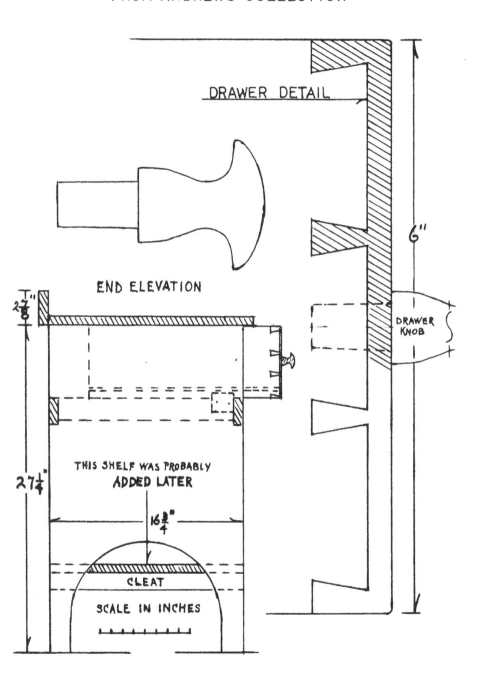

DRAWER DETAIL

END ELEVATION

DRAWER KNOB

6"

27 7/8"

27 1/4"

THIS SHELF WAS PROBABLY ADDED LATER

16 3/4"

CLEAT

SCALE IN INCHES

DROP-LEAF TABLE

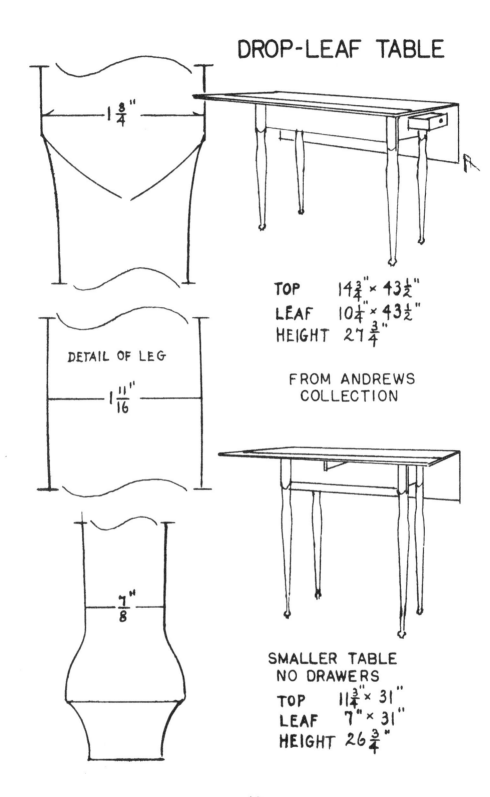

$1\frac{3}{4}$"

DETAIL OF LEG

$1\frac{11}{16}$"

$\frac{7}{8}$"

TOP $14\frac{3}{4}$"× $43\frac{1}{2}$"
LEAF $10\frac{1}{4}$"× $43\frac{1}{2}$"
HEIGHT $27\frac{3}{4}$"

FROM ANDREWS
COLLECTION

SMALLER TABLE
NO DRAWERS
TOP $11\frac{3}{4}$"× 31"
LEAF   7"× 31"
HEIGHT $26\frac{3}{4}$"

18

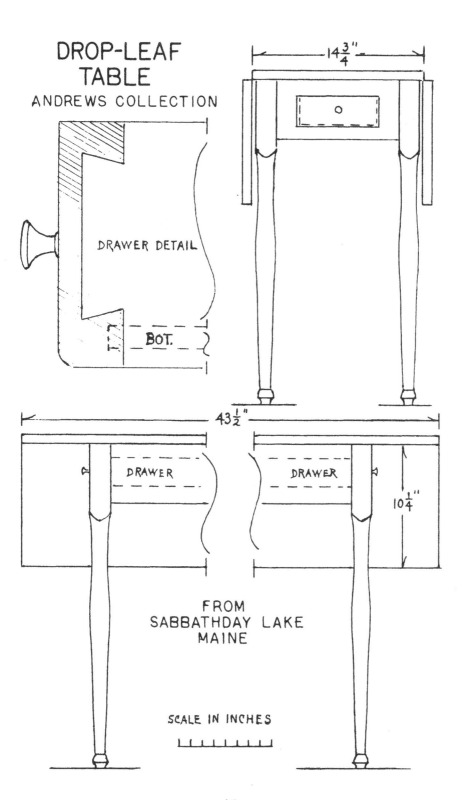

DROP-LEAF
TABLE
ANDREWS COLLECTION

$14\frac{3}{4}''$

DRAWER DETAIL

BOT.

$43\frac{1}{2}''$

DRAWER

DRAWER

$10\frac{1}{4}''$

FROM
SABBATHDAY LAKE
MAINE

SCALE IN INCHES

19

SMALL TABLE
LEGS OF CHERRY
TOP, FRAME AND DRAWER OF CHESTNUT

FROM ANDREWS COLLECTION

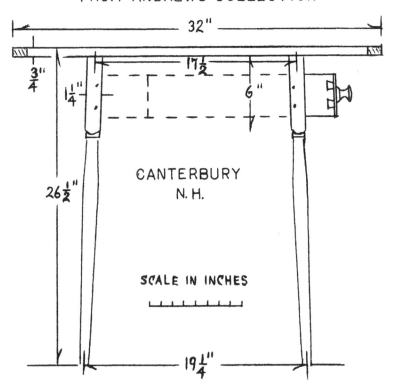

32"

3/4"

1 1/4"

17 1/2

6"

26 1/2"

CANTERBURY
N. H.

SCALE IN INCHES

19 1/4"

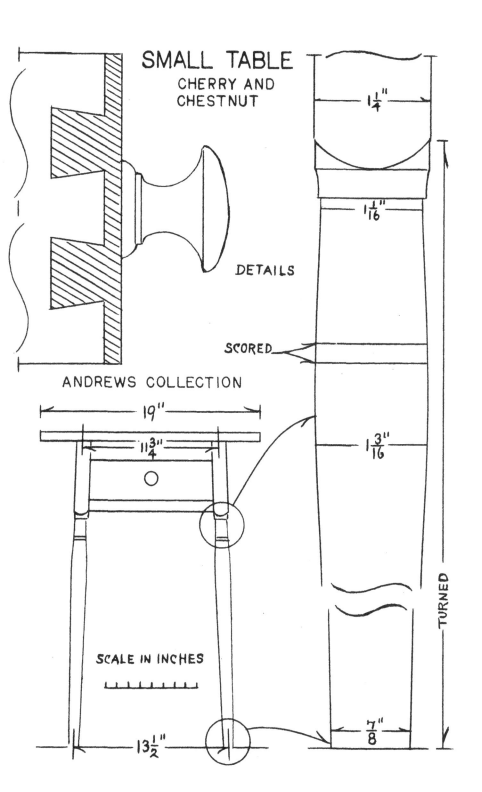

SMALL TABLE
CHERRY AND CHESTNUT

$1\frac{1}{4}''$

DETAILS

$1\frac{1}{16}''$

SCORED

ANDREWS COLLECTION

19''

$11\frac{3}{4}''$

$1\frac{3}{16}''$

SCALE IN INCHES

TURNED

$\frac{7}{8}''$

$13\frac{1}{2}''$

21

TABLE
BIRD'S-EYE MAPLE
THE SHAKER MUSEUM,
OLD CHATHAM, N.Y.

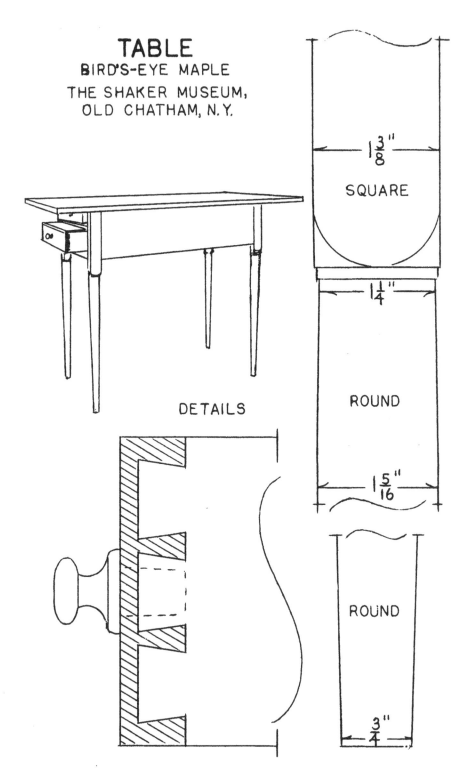

SQUARE

$1\frac{3}{8}''$

$1\frac{1}{4}''$

ROUND

$1\frac{5}{16}''$

ROUND

$\frac{3}{4}''$

DETAILS

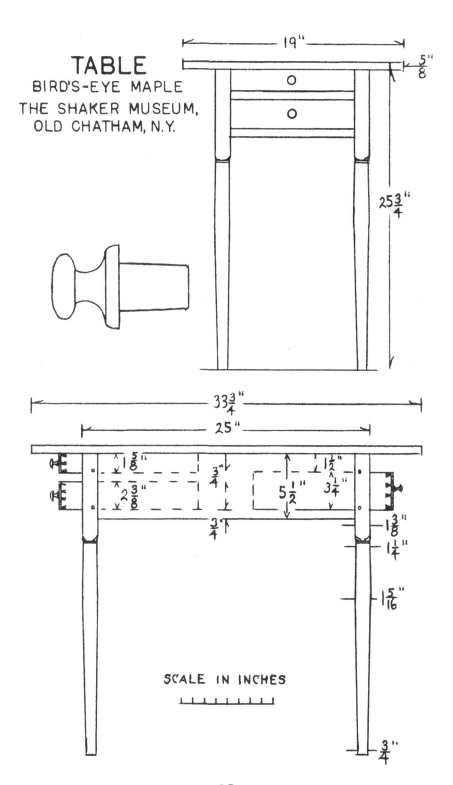

TABLE
BIRD'S-EYE MAPLE
THE SHAKER MUSEUM,
OLD CHATHAM, N.Y.

19"

$\frac{5}{8}$"

$25\frac{3}{4}$"

$33\frac{3}{4}$"

25"

$1\frac{5}{8}$"

$\frac{3}{4}$"

$1\frac{1}{2}$"

$2\frac{3}{8}$"

$5\frac{1}{2}$"

$3\frac{1}{4}$"

$\frac{3}{4}$"

$1\frac{3}{8}$"

$1\frac{1}{4}$"

$1\frac{5}{16}$"

$\frac{3}{4}$"

SCALE IN INCHES

PEG-LEG STAND

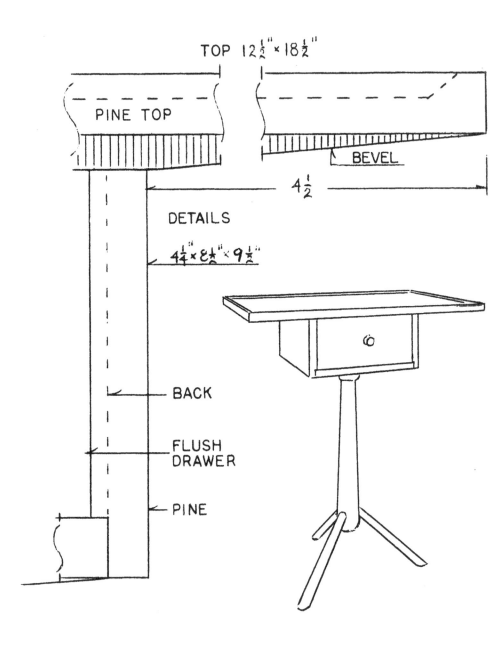

TOP $12\frac{1}{2}" \times 18\frac{1}{2}"$

PINE TOP

BEVEL

$4\frac{1}{2}$

DETAILS

$4\frac{1}{4}" \times 8\frac{1}{8}" \times 9\frac{1}{2}"$

BACK

FLUSH DRAWER

PINE

PEG-LEG STAND

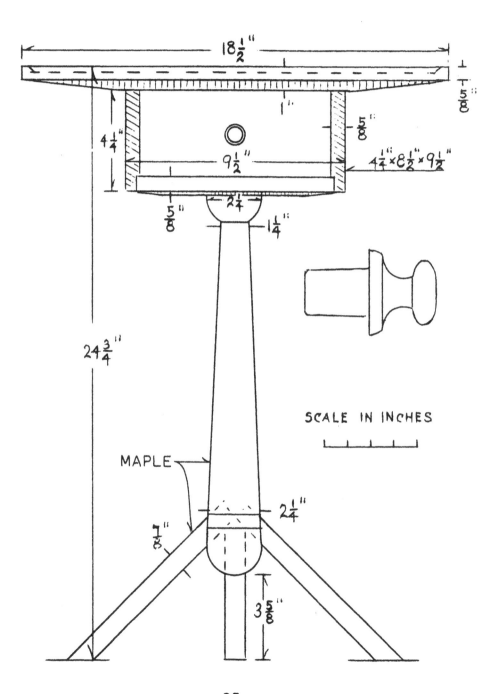

$18\frac{1}{2}$″

$\frac{5}{8}$″

1″

$4\frac{1}{4}$″

$\frac{5}{8}$″

$9\frac{1}{2}$″

$4\frac{1}{4}$″×$8\frac{1}{2}$″×$9\frac{1}{2}$″

$2\frac{1}{4}$

$\frac{5}{8}$″

$1\frac{1}{4}$″

$24\frac{3}{4}$″

SCALE IN INCHES

MAPLE

$2\frac{1}{4}$″

$\frac{7}{8}$″

$3\frac{5}{8}$″

25

DETAIL OF SHAFT

$1\frac{1}{8}''$

$1\frac{1}{16}''$

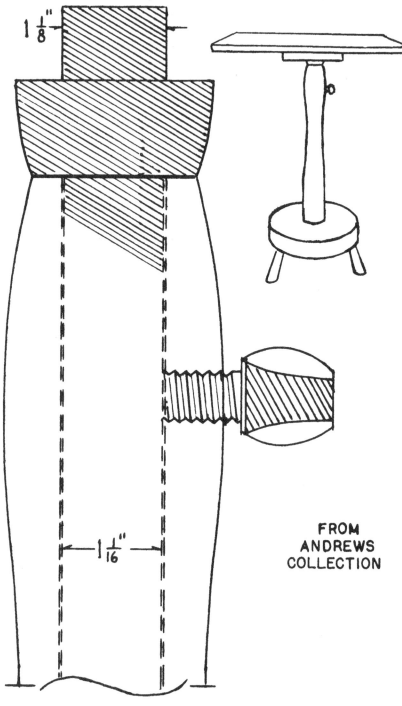

FROM
ANDREWS
COLLECTION

EARLY STAND
WITH ADJUSTABLE TOP

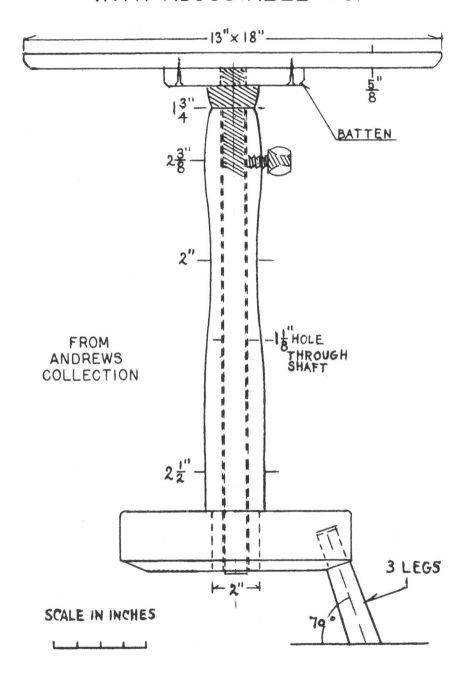

13" × 18"

5/8"

BATTEN

1 3/4"

2 3/8"

2"

FROM
ANDREWS
COLLECTION

1 1/8" HOLE
THROUGH
SHAFT

2 1/2"

3 LEGS

2"

SCALE IN INCHES

79°

STAND WITH ADJUSTABLE TOP
MAPLE AND PINE

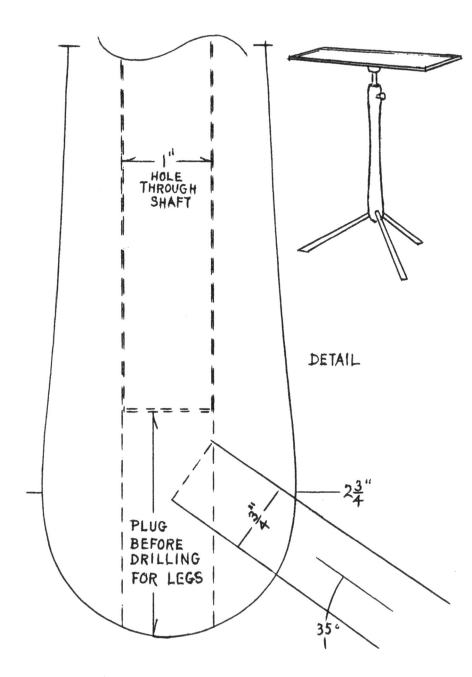

1" HOLE THROUGH SHAFT

DETAIL

PLUG BEFORE DRILLING FOR LEGS

$2\frac{3}{4}"$

$\frac{3}{4}"$

35°

STAND WITH ADJUSTABLE TOP
SHAFT AND LEGS OF MAPLE TOP OF PINE

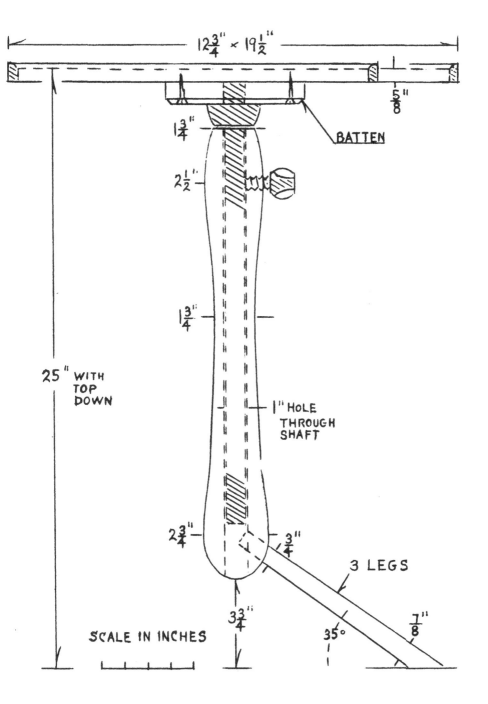

$12\frac{3}{4}"$ × $19\frac{1}{2}"$

$\frac{5}{8}"$

BATTEN

$1\frac{3}{4}"$

$2\frac{1}{2}"$

$1\frac{3}{4}"$

25" WITH TOP DOWN

1" HOLE THROUGH SHAFT

$2\frac{3}{4}"$

$\frac{3}{4}"$

3 LEGS

$\frac{7}{8}"$

$3\frac{3}{4}"$

35°

SCALE IN INCHES

29

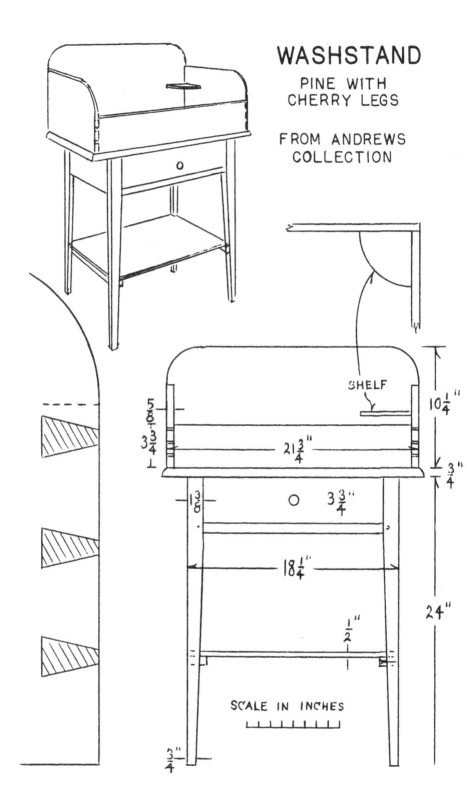

WASHSTAND
PINE WITH
CHERRY LEGS

FROM ANDREWS
COLLECTION

SHELF

$10\frac{1}{4}$"

$\frac{5}{8}$

$3\frac{3}{4}$

$21\frac{3}{4}$"

$\frac{3}{4}$"

$1\frac{3}{8}$

$3\frac{3}{4}$"

$18\frac{1}{4}$"

24"

$\frac{1}{2}$"

SCALE IN INCHES

$\frac{3}{4}$"

WASHSTAND

PINE WITH CHERRY LEGS

FROM ANDREWS COLLECTION

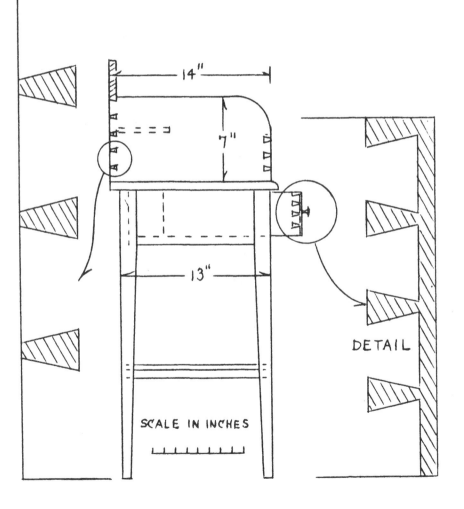

14"

7"

13"

DETAIL

SCALE IN INCHES

WASHSTAND

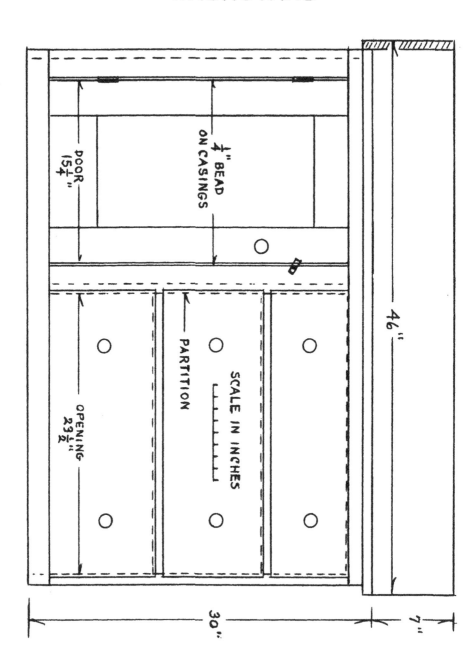

FROM ANDREWS COLLECTION

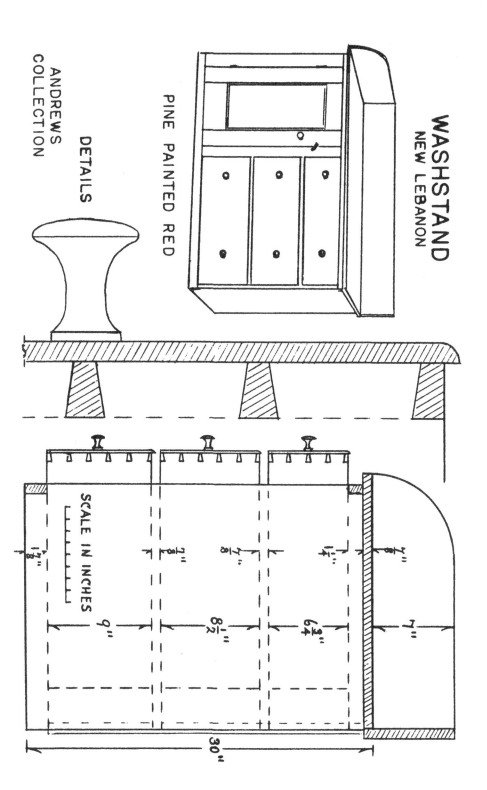

WASHSTAND
NEW LEBANON

PINE PAINTED RED

DETAILS

ANDREWS
COLLECTION

SCALE IN INCHES

$\frac{7}{8}$"

$\frac{7}{8}$"

$\frac{1}{4}$"

$1\frac{1}{4}$"

$\frac{7}{8}$"

$1\frac{7}{8}$"

9"

$8\frac{1}{2}$"

$6\frac{3}{4}$"

7"

30"

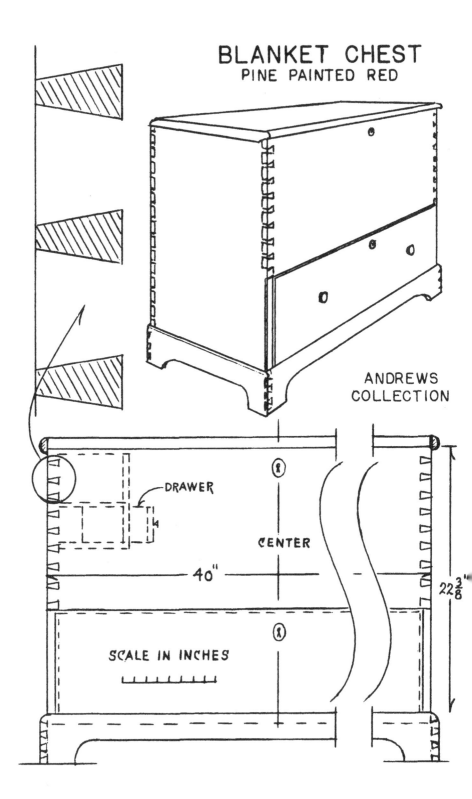

BLANKET CHEST
PINE PAINTED RED

ANDREWS
COLLECTION

DRAWER

CENTER

40"

$22\frac{3}{8}$"

SCALE IN INCHES

BLANKET CHEST
PINE PAINTED RED

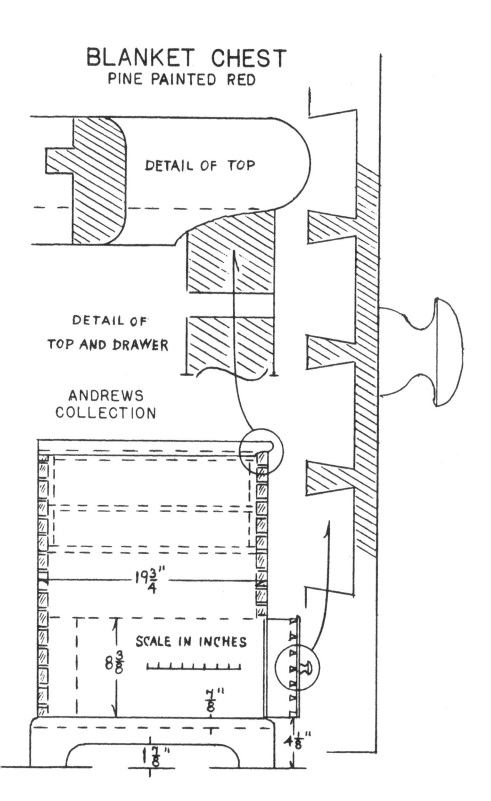

DETAIL OF TOP

DETAIL OF
TOP AND DRAWER

ANDREWS
COLLECTION

$19\frac{3}{4}$"

$8\frac{3}{8}$"

SCALE IN INCHES

$\frac{7}{8}$"

$1\frac{7}{8}$"

$4\frac{1}{8}$"

WOOD-BOX
PINE, STAINED RED

FROM
ANDREWS
COLLECTION

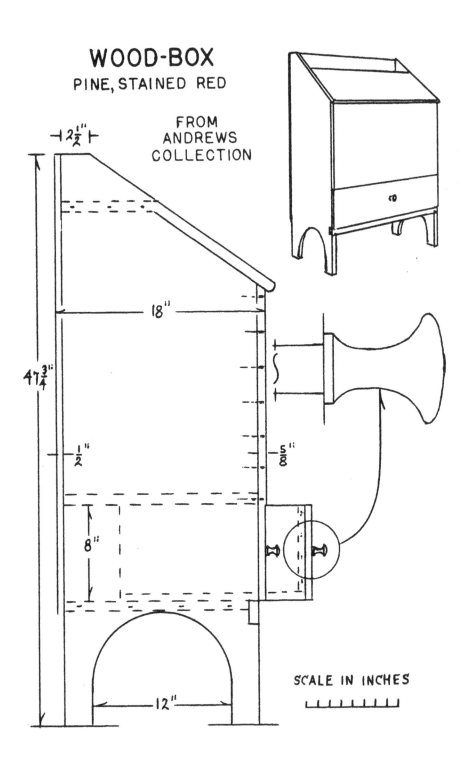

$2\frac{1}{2}''$

18"

$47\frac{3}{4}''$

$\frac{1}{2}''$

$\frac{5}{8}''$

8"

12"

SCALE IN INCHES

WOOD-BOX
MADE FOR THE MINISTRY CANTERBURY N.H.

FROM ANDREWS COLLECTION

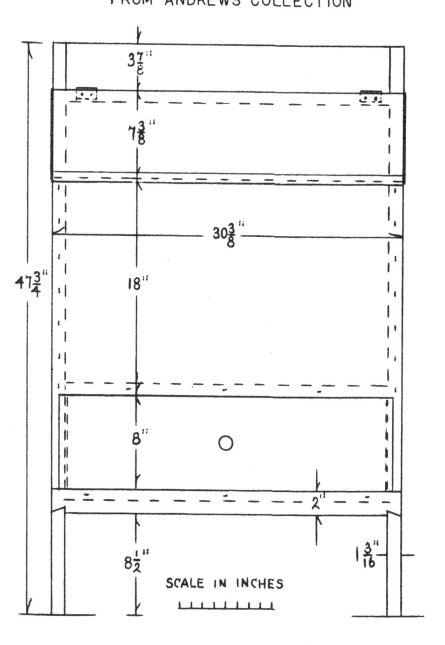

$3\frac{7}{8}$"

$7\frac{3}{8}$"

$30\frac{3}{8}$"

$47\frac{3}{4}$"

18"

8"

2"

$8\frac{1}{2}$"

$1\frac{3}{16}$"

SCALE IN INCHES

2 DRAWER UTILITY CHEST

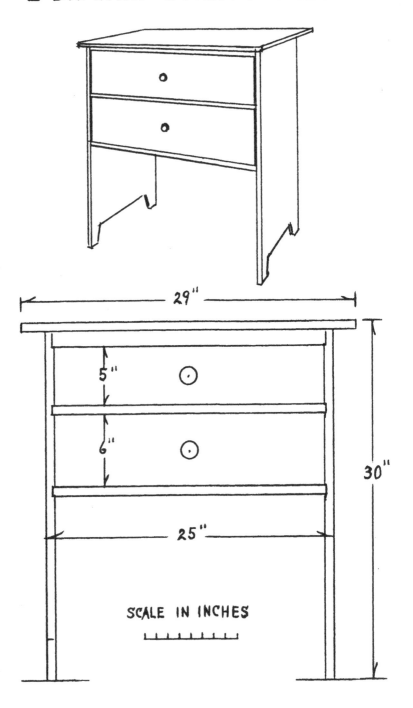

29"

5"

6"

30"

25"

SCALE IN INCHES

38

2 DRAWER UTILITY CHEST

FROM ANDREWS COLLECTION

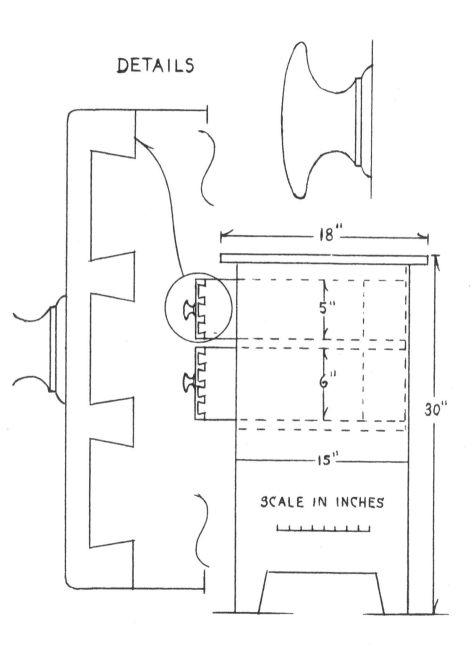

DETAILS

18"

5"

6"

30"

15"

SCALE IN INCHES

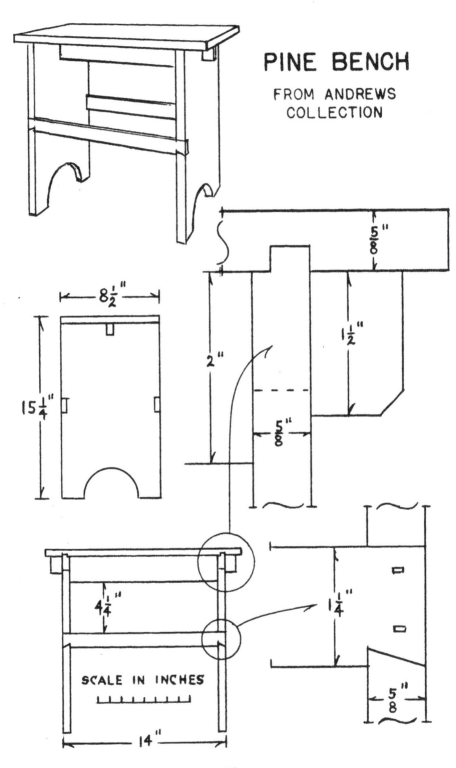

PINE BENCH

FROM ANDREWS
COLLECTION

$8\frac{1}{2}"$

$15\frac{1}{4}"$

$\frac{5}{8}"$

$2"$

$1\frac{1}{2}"$

$\frac{5}{8}"$

$4\frac{1}{4}"$

$1\frac{1}{4}"$

$\frac{5}{8}"$

SCALE IN INCHES

$14"$

40

KITCHEN BENCH
HANCOCK SHAKER VILLAGE, HANCOCK MASS.

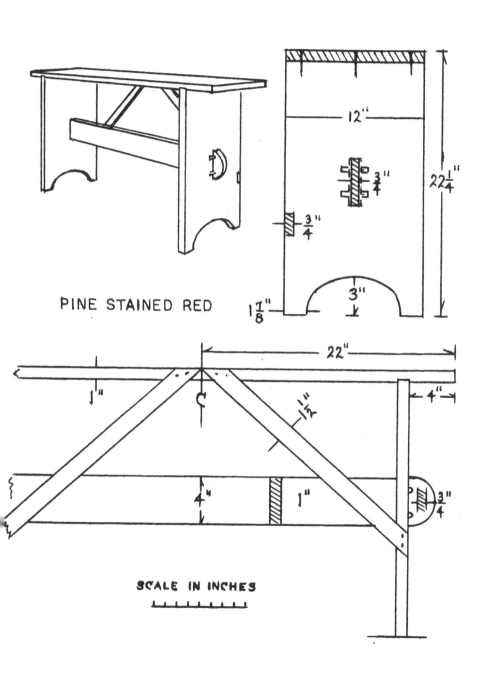

PINE STAINED RED

12"

22¼"

3"/4

3"/4

1⅞"

3"

22"

1"

4"

1½"

C

4"

1"

3"/4

SCALE IN INCHES

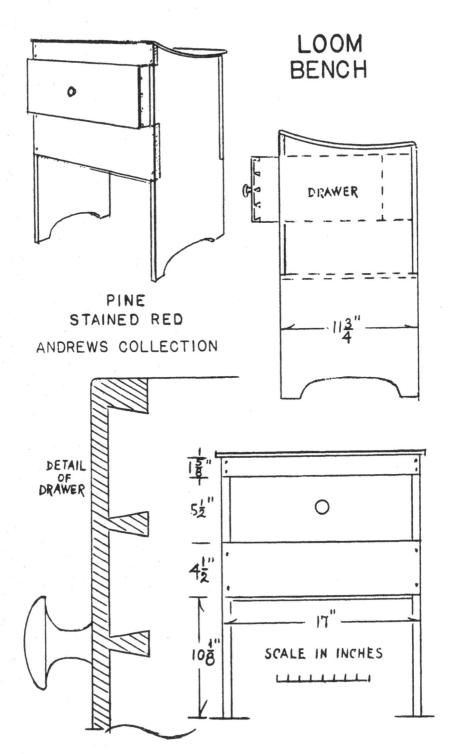

LOOM BENCH

PINE
STAINED RED

ANDREWS COLLECTION

DRAWER

$11\frac{3}{4}''$

DETAIL OF DRAWER

$1\frac{5}{8}''$

$5\frac{1}{2}''$

$4\frac{1}{2}''$

$10\frac{1}{8}''$

$17''$

SCALE IN INCHES

LOOM STOOL

STOOL OF PINE
BACK OF BIRCH
STAINED RED

ANDREWS COLLECTION

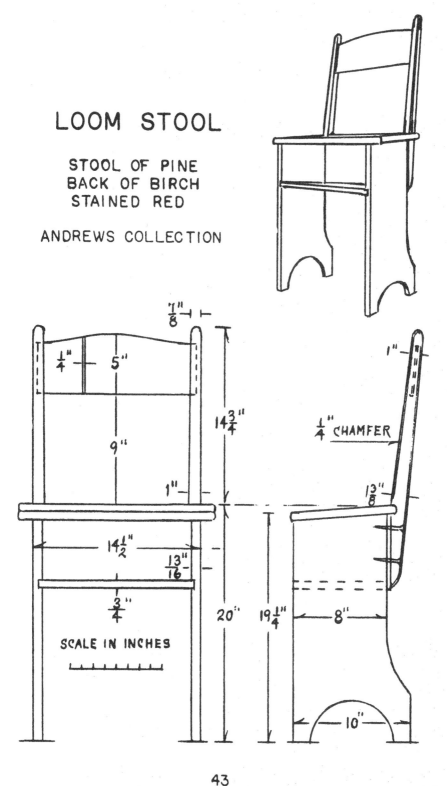

SCALE IN INCHES

43

STEP-STOOL

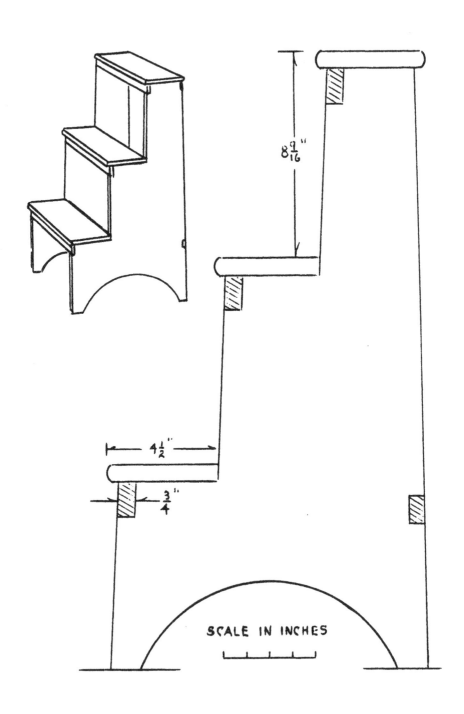

$8\frac{9}{16}''$

$4\frac{1}{2}''$

$\frac{3}{4}''$

SCALE IN INCHES

44

STEP-STOOL

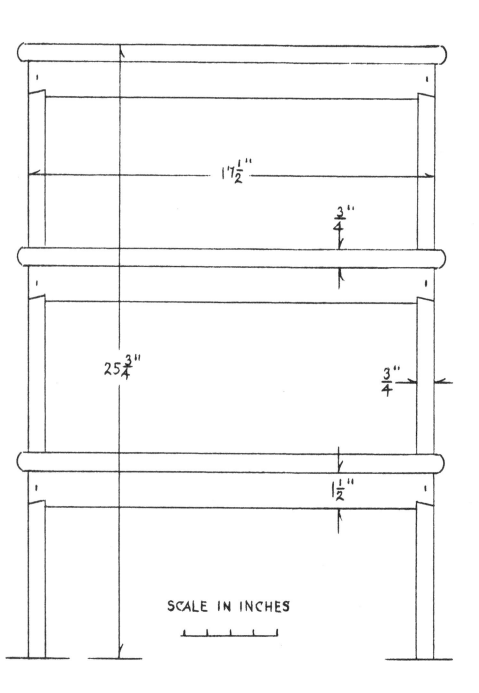

$17\frac{1}{2}"$

$\frac{3}{4}"$

$25\frac{3}{4}"$

$\frac{3}{4}"$

$1\frac{1}{2}"$

SCALE IN INCHES

REVOLVING STOOL

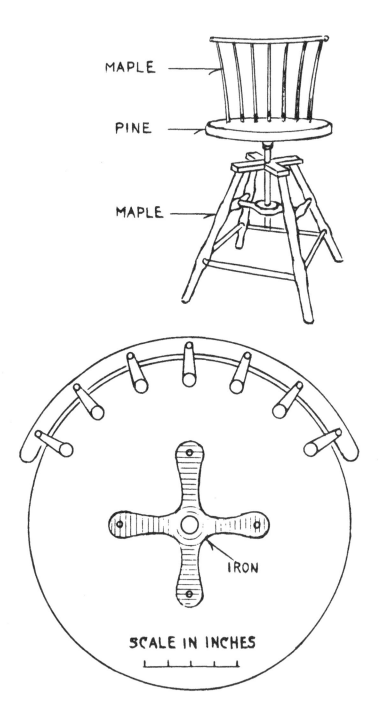

MAPLE

PINE

MAPLE

IRON

SCALE IN INCHES

REVOLVING STOOL

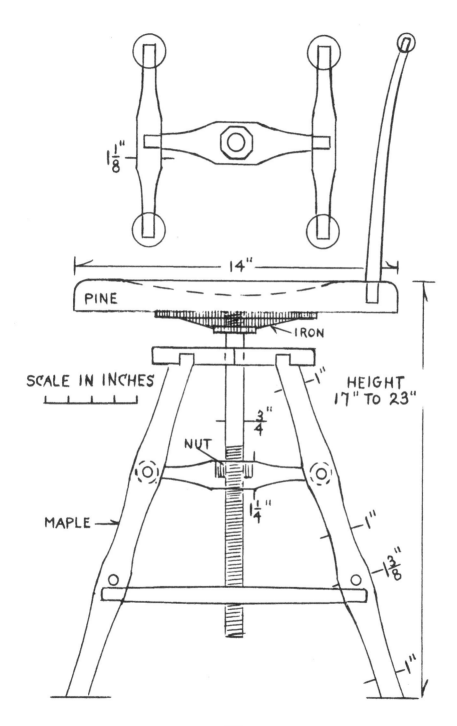

$1\frac{1}{8}$"

14"

PINE

IRON

SCALE IN INCHES

$\frac{3}{4}$"

NUT

$1\frac{1}{4}$"

MAPLE

1"

HEIGHT
17" TO 23"

1"

$1\frac{3}{8}$"

1"

STOOL MT. LEBANON

THE SHAKER MUSEUM
OLD CHATHAM, N.Y.

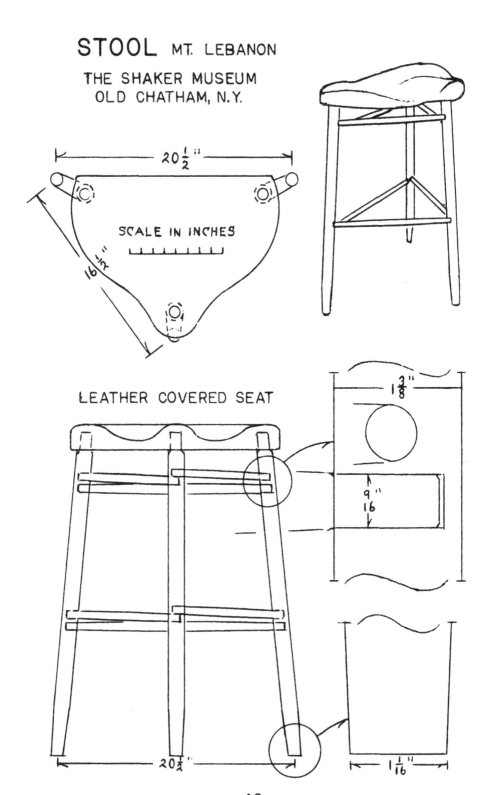

$20\frac{1}{2}$"

SCALE IN INCHES

$16\frac{1}{2}$"

LEATHER COVERED SEAT

$1\frac{3}{8}$"

$\frac{9}{16}$"

$20\frac{1}{2}$"

$1\frac{1}{16}$"

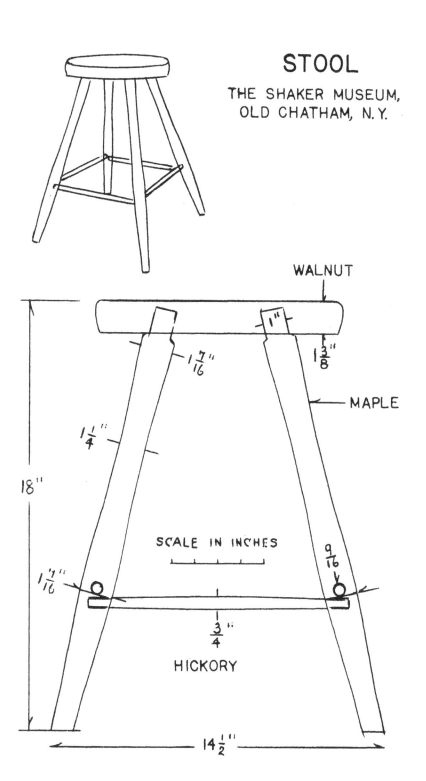

STOOL

THE SHAKER MUSEUM,
OLD CHATHAM, N.Y.

WALNUT

1"

$1\frac{3}{8}$"

$1\frac{7}{16}$"

MAPLE

$1\frac{1}{4}$"

18"

SCALE IN INCHES

$\frac{9}{16}$

$1\frac{7}{16}$"

$\frac{3}{4}$"

HICKORY

$14\frac{1}{2}$"

ELDER ROBERT M. WAGAN
CHAIRMAKER

Illustrated Catalogue

AND

PRICE LIST

OF

Shakers' ✲ Chairs,

MANUFACTURED BY THE

Society ✲ of ✲ Shakers.

R. M. WAGAN & CO,

MOUNT LEBANON, N. Y.

51

HANCOCK
ARMCHAIR

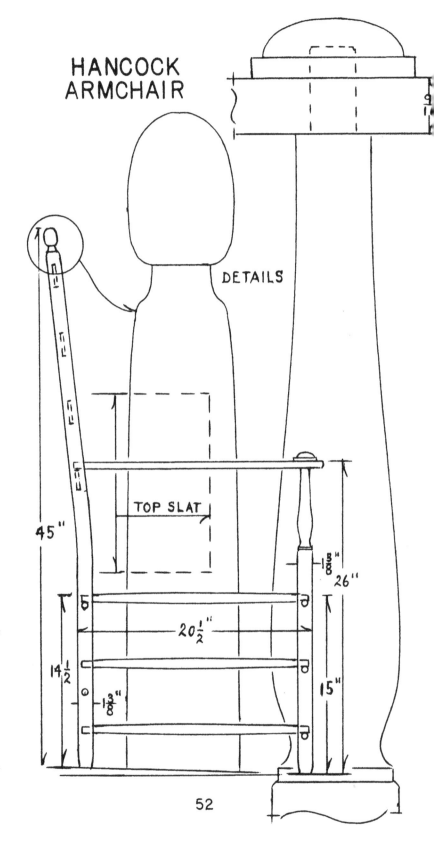

DETAILS

TOP SLAT

45"

$1\frac{3}{8}$"

26"

$20\frac{1}{2}$"

$14\frac{1}{2}$

$1\frac{3}{8}$"

15"

52

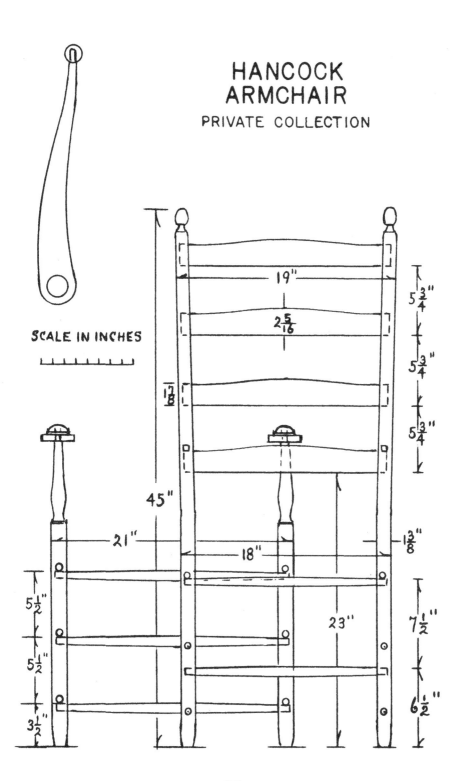

HANCOCK
ARMCHAIR
PRIVATE COLLECTION

SCALE IN INCHES

19"

$2\frac{5}{16}$

$5\frac{3}{4}$"

$5\frac{3}{4}$"

$5\frac{3}{4}$"

$1\frac{7}{8}$

45"

21"

18"

$1\frac{3}{8}$"

$5\frac{1}{2}$"

$5\frac{1}{2}$"

$3\frac{1}{2}$"

23"

$7\frac{1}{2}$"

$6\frac{1}{2}$"

COUNTER
CHAIR

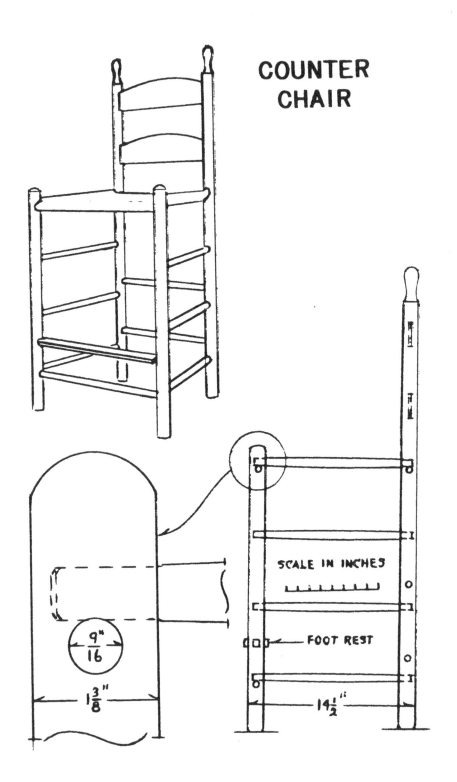

SCALE IN INCHES

FOOT REST

$\frac{9''}{16}$

$1\frac{3}{8}''$

$14\frac{1}{2}''$

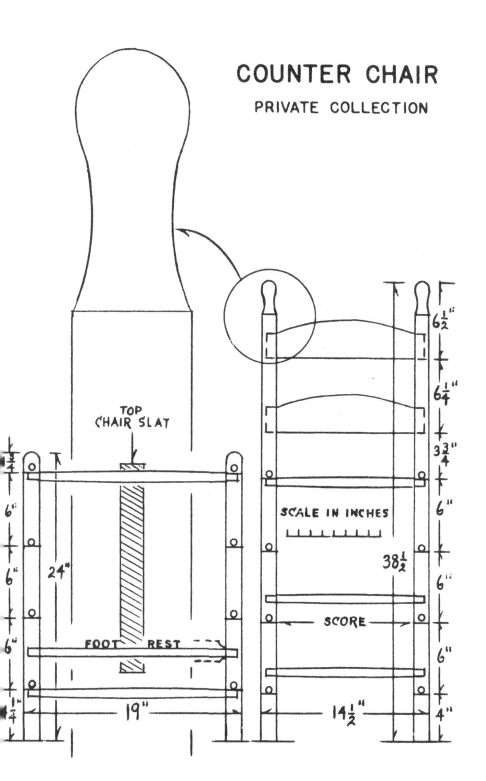

COUNTER CHAIR
PRIVATE COLLECTION

TOP
CHAIR SLAT

SCALE IN INCHES

FOOT REST

SCORE

$6\frac{1}{2}$"

$6\frac{1}{4}$"

$3\frac{3}{4}$"

6"

6"

6"

4"

$38\frac{1}{2}$

$14\frac{1}{2}$"

$1\frac{1}{4}$"

6"

6"

6"

$1\frac{1}{4}$"

24"

19"

BRETHREN'S ROCKER
NEW LEBANON N.Y.

PRIVATE COLLECTION

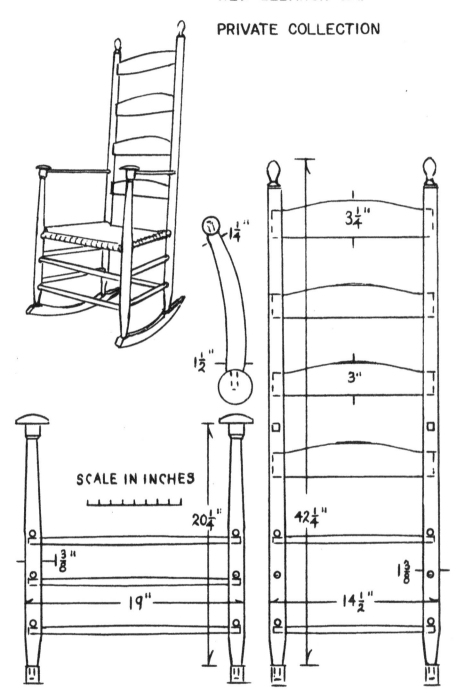

$3\frac{1}{4}$"

$1\frac{1}{4}$"

$1\frac{1}{2}$"

3"

SCALE IN INCHES

$20\frac{1}{4}$"

$42\frac{1}{4}$"

$1\frac{3}{8}$"

19"

$1\frac{3}{8}$"

$14\frac{1}{2}$"

BRETHREN'S ROCKER
NEW LEBANON N.Y.
PRIVATE COLLECTION

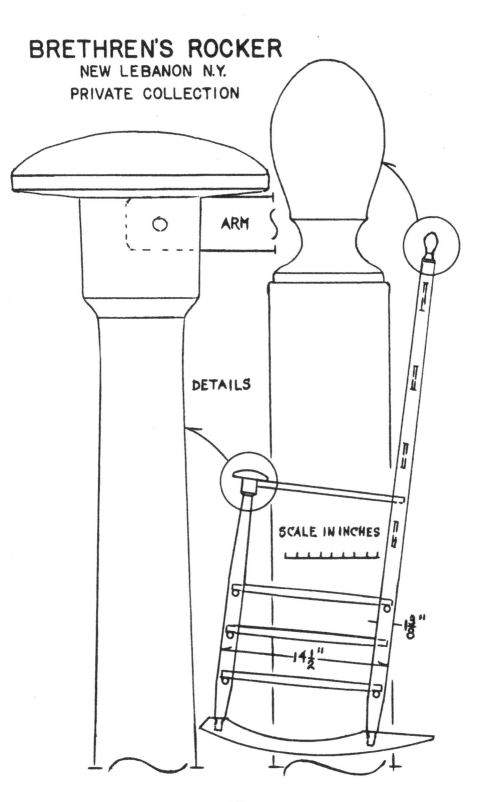

ARM

DETAILS

SCALE IN INCHES

$14\frac{1}{2}$"

CHAIR FINIALS

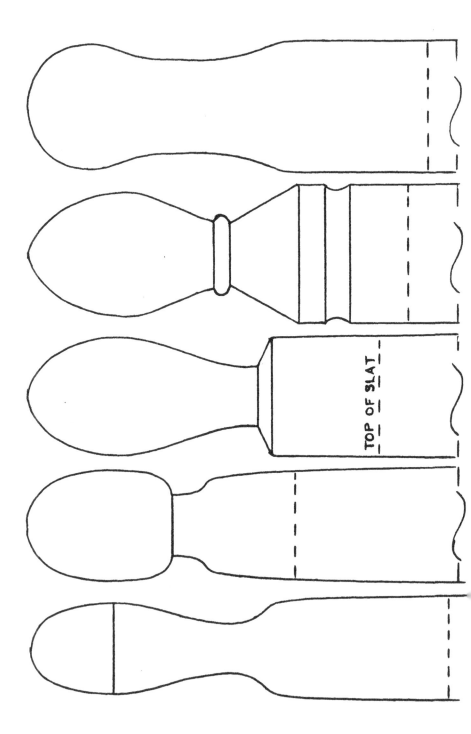

TOP OF SLAT

CHAIR MUSHROOMS
AND TILTING BUTTONS

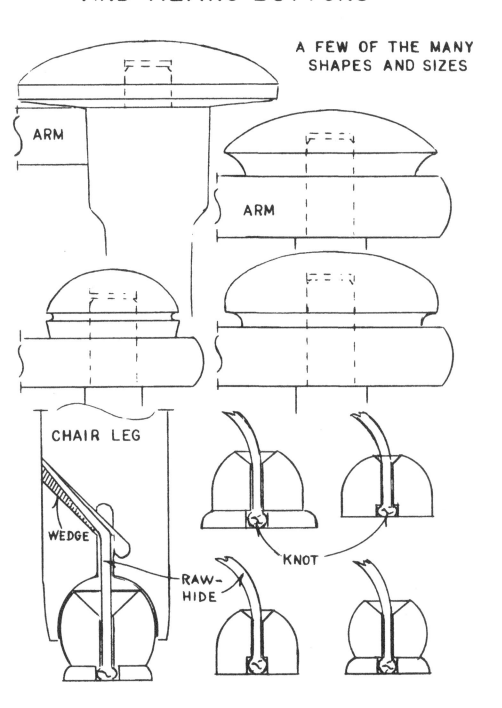

A FEW OF THE MANY
SHAPES AND SIZES

ARM

ARM

CHAIR LEG

WEDGE

RAW-
HIDE

KNOT

DRAWER PULLS

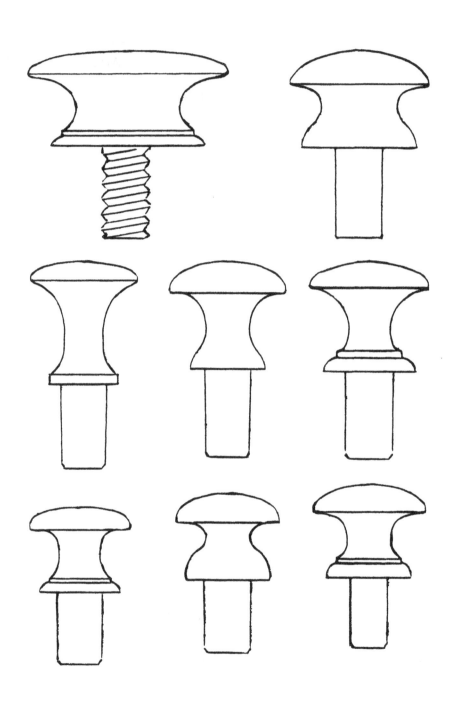

BED CASTERS

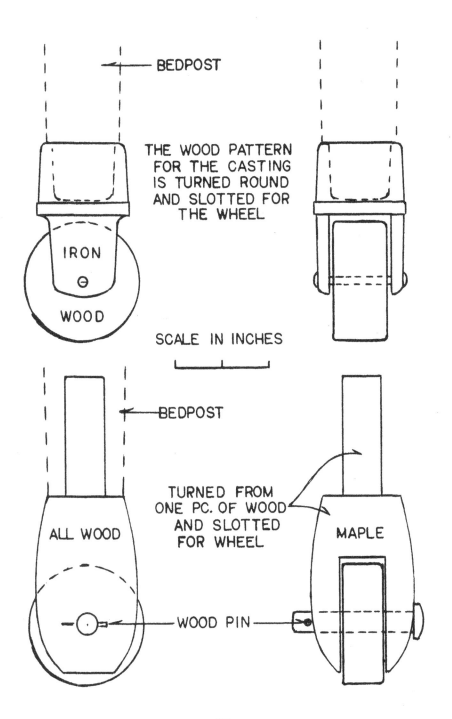

BEDPOST

THE WOOD PATTERN
FOR THE CASTING
IS TURNED ROUND
AND SLOTTED FOR
THE WHEEL

IRON

WOOD

SCALE IN INCHES

BEDPOST

TURNED FROM
ONE PC. OF WOOD
AND SLOTTED
FOR WHEEL

ALL WOOD

MAPLE

WOOD PIN

HANGING SHELF

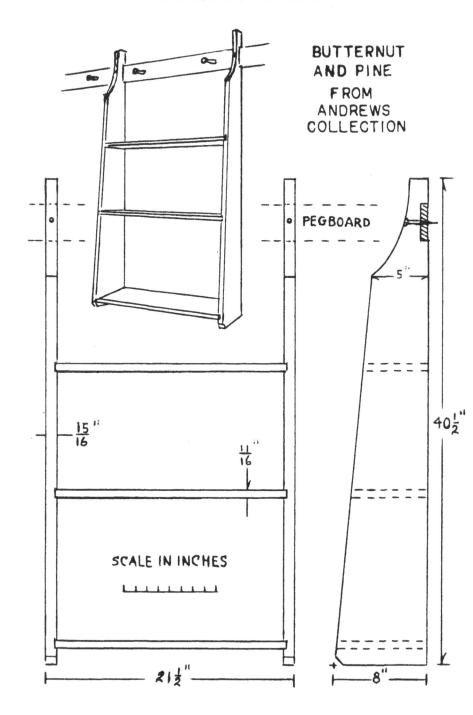

BUTTERNUT
AND PINE
FROM
ANDREWS
COLLECTION

PEGBOARD

5"

40$\frac{1}{2}$"

15$\frac{1}{16}$"

11$\frac{1}{16}$"

SCALE IN INCHES

21$\frac{1}{2}$"

8"

SMALL WALL CUPBOARD

HANCOCK SHAKER VILLAGE, HANCOCK MASS.

DETAILS

PINE

$\frac{7}{16}" \times \frac{3}{4}"$ BATTENS

$11\frac{1}{8}"$

SCALE IN INCHES

$\frac{1}{4}"$

$4\frac{1}{2}"$

$13"$

$\frac{3}{8}"$

$\frac{1}{4}"$

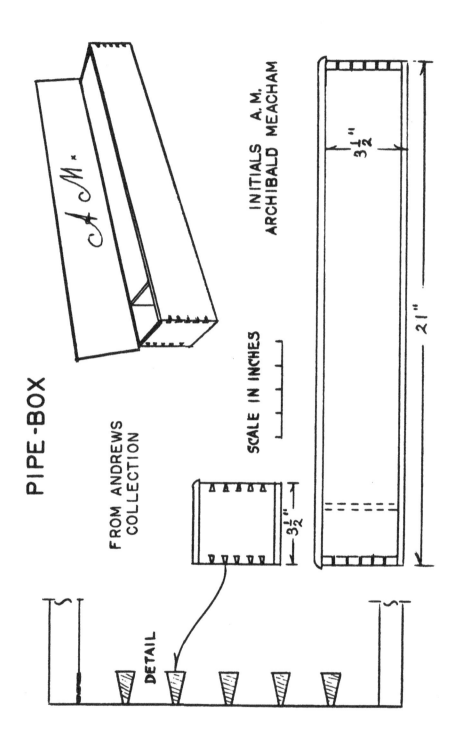

PIPE-BOX

FROM ANDREWS COLLECTION

INITIALS A. M.
ARCHIBALD MEACHAM

SCALE IN INCHES

DETAIL

$3\frac{1}{2}''$

$3\frac{1}{2}''$

21"

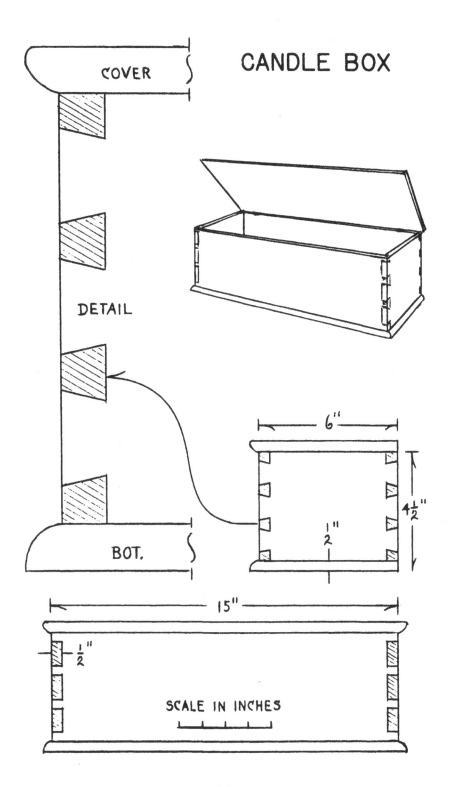

CANDLE BOX

COVER

DETAIL

BOT.

6"

4½"

1"
2

15"

1"
2

SCALE IN INCHES

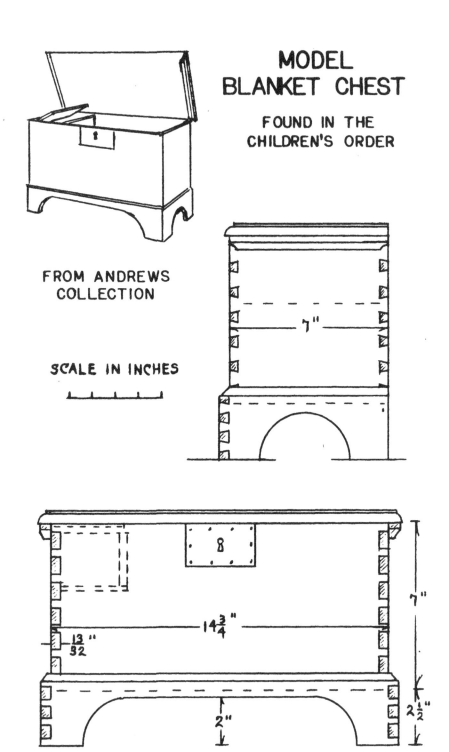

MODEL
BLANKET CHEST

FOUND IN THE
CHILDREN'S ORDER

FROM ANDREWS
COLLECTION

SCALE IN INCHES

7"

8

14¾"

13/32"

7"

2"

2½"

WALNUT TRAY

NEW LEBANON, N.Y.   PRIVATE COLLECTION

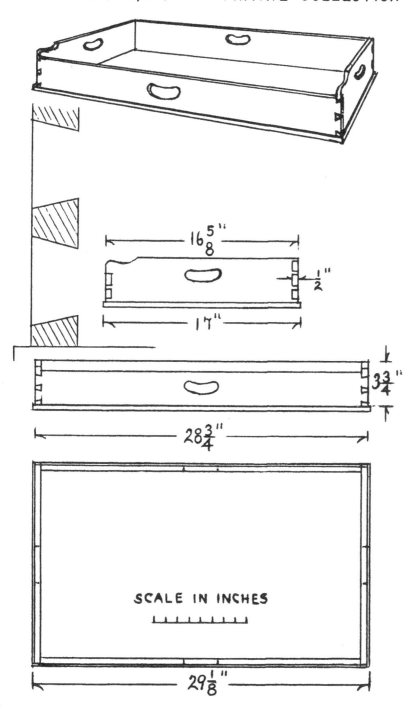

$16\frac{5}{8}$"

$\frac{1}{2}$"

17"

$3\frac{3}{4}$"

$28\frac{3}{4}$"

SCALE IN INCHES

$29\frac{1}{8}$"

SCOOP
PRIVATE COLLECTION

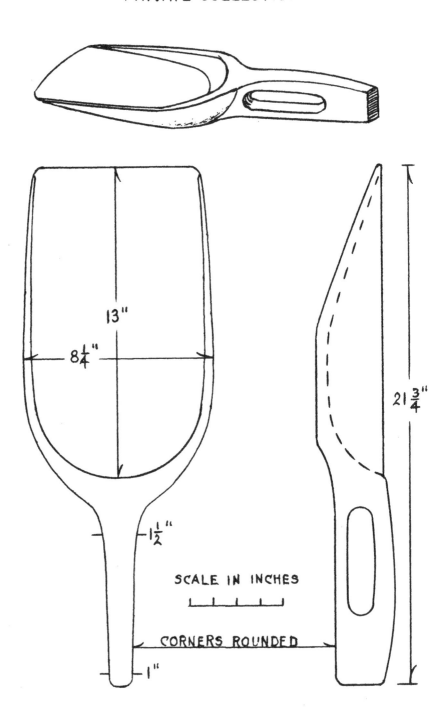

13"

8¼"

1½"

21¾"

SCALE IN INCHES

CORNERS ROUNDED

1"

MORTAR AND PESTLE
THE SHAKER MUSEUM, OLD CHATHAM, N.Y.

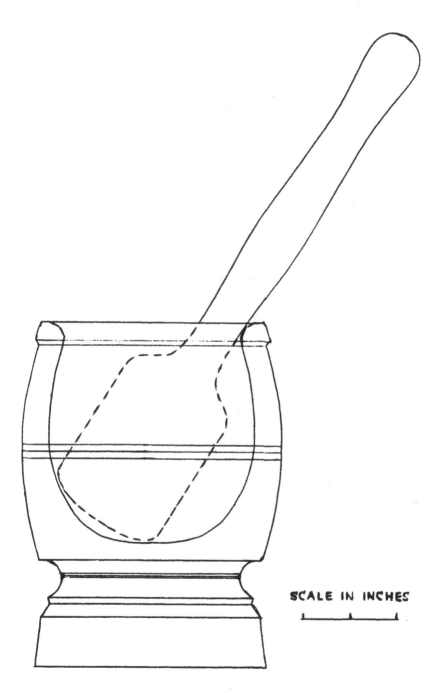

SCALE IN INCHES

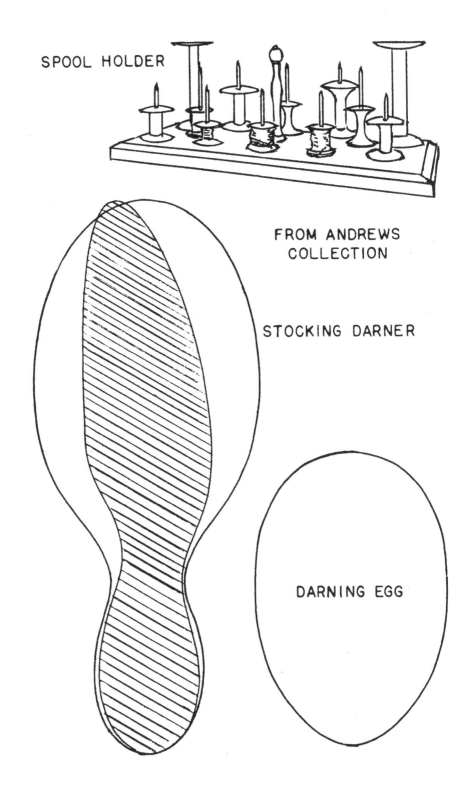

SPOOL HOLDER

FROM ANDREWS
COLLECTION

STOCKING DARNER

DARNING EGG

THUMB AND MITTEN DARNER

FROM
ANDREWS
COLLECTION

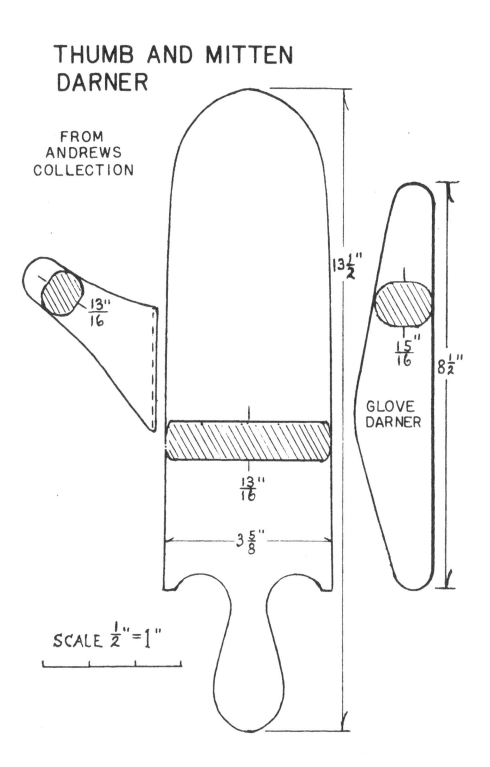

$13\frac{1}{2}$"

$\frac{13"}{16}$

$\frac{15"}{16}$

$8\frac{1}{2}$"

GLOVE
DARNER

$\frac{13"}{16}$

$3\frac{5}{8}$"

SCALE $\frac{1}{2}$"$=1$"

71

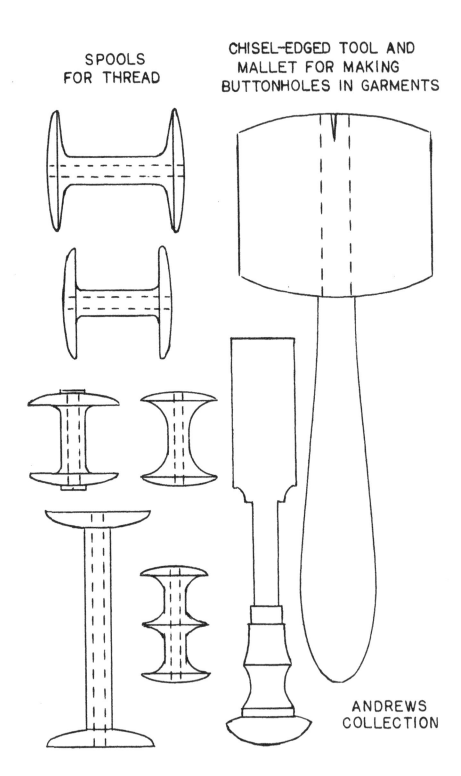

SPOOLS
FOR THREAD

CHISEL-EDGED TOOL AND
MALLET FOR MAKING
BUTTONHOLES IN GARMENTS

ANDREWS
COLLECTION

72

SHAKER MADE ITEMS

1 DARNER
2 BONNET PLEATER
3   "   "
4 SPOOL FOR THREAD

PRIVATE COLLECTION

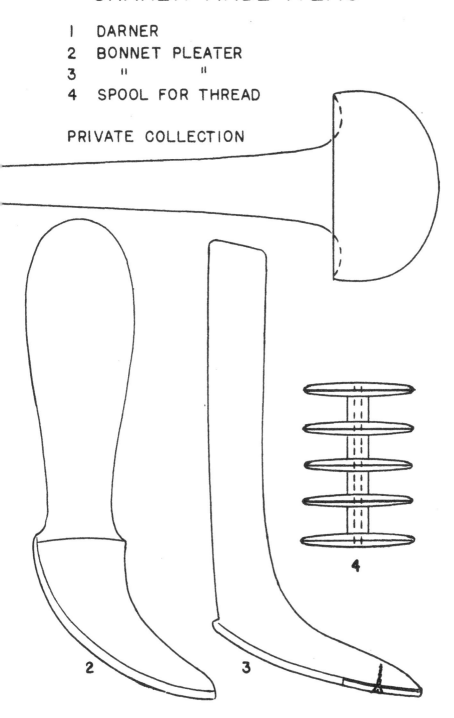

73

MT. LEBANON STOVE

DOUBLE FOR MORE EFFICIENT HEATING

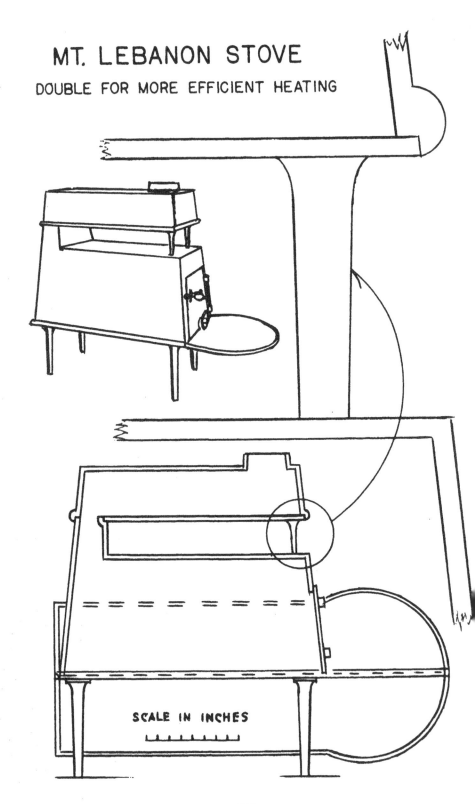

SCALE IN INCHES

MT. LEBANON STOVE

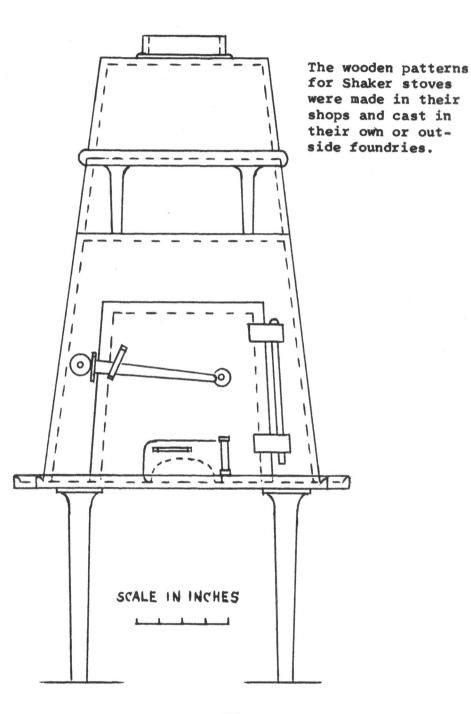

The wooden patterns
for Shaker stoves
were made in their
shops and cast in
their own or out-
side foundries.

SCALE IN INCHES

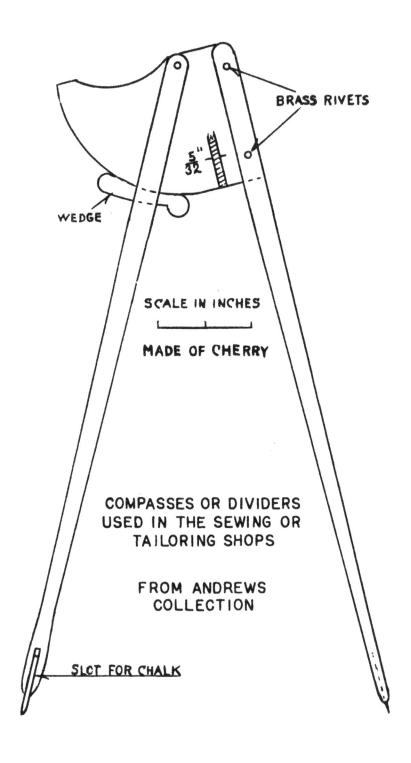

BRASS RIVETS

$\frac{5}{32}$"

WEDGE

SCALE IN INCHES

MADE OF CHERRY

COMPASSES OR DIVIDERS
USED IN THE SEWING OR
TAILORING SHOPS

FROM ANDREWS
COLLECTION

SLOT FOR CHALK

76

Washstand — page 33

Bake-Room Table – page 16

Washstand – page 30

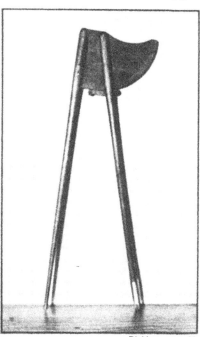

Dividers – page 76

Drop-Leaf Table — page 18

Pine Table — page 14

Blanket Chest — page 34

Desk — page 4

Wood-Box — page 36

Pine Bench — page 40

Loom Bench — page 42

Spool Holder — page 70

INDEX

Asterisks after plate numbers refer to drawings made from pieces in the collection of Dr. and Mrs. Edward Deming Andrews.

Shop Drawings
of Shaker Furniture
and Woodenware

Volume 3

Measured Drawings
by Ejner Handberg

CONTENTS

NOTES TO THE CRAFTSMAN OR COLLECTOR

The Shakers used local woods for their furniture mainly from their own land, and all lumber was carefully dried. In the Northeast, large case furniture such as cupboards, chests of drawers, blanket chests, wood boxes and washstands were nearly always made of Eastern white pine. Tables, stands and desks (both writing desks and sewing desks) were often constructed of mixed woods such as cherry, maple, butternut and others. Maple, birch and cherry were used in all pieces requiring strength and withstanding wear such as chairs and stools, of which there were many kinds. Hickory and ash were used for parts which were to be bent.Sometimes candlestands,work stands and sewing stands were made of cherry, maple or birch with a pine top. One feature in Shaker furniture and woodenware was the use of quarter-sawn, edge-grained pine which is less apt to cup or warp than flat-grained boards.

Occasionally pieces can be seen made entirely of walnut, chestnut, butternut and also, but not so often, one can find a small stand, table or chair made of birds-eye maple, curly maple or tiger maple. It is not unusual to see a piece of Shaker furniture where more than one kind of wood was used, as for example, the table legs of cherry, the frame or skirt of maple and the top of pine.

The making of freestanding or movable pieces for use in the early workshops and dwelling houses probably preceded the cupboards and drawers which were permanently built into the walls of many buildings. These were usually six to eight feet high and in no particular pattern, sometimes numbering a hundred or more cupboards and drawers on one wall.

Their furniture was not designed and made for show. There were no fancy turnings or mouldings; everything was designed and made for a purpose, for the Shakers had only utility in mind. There is a Shaker saying "that which has the highest use possesses the greatest beauty."

The eventual result was an original and very simple but beautiful style, that was all their own. From the beginning they continued to improve their methods looking only for strength and lightness. Yet there was always a freedom to make new designs and, because of this, it is seldom possible to find, for example, two trestle tables or two sewing desks which are alike.

An Elder from New Lebanon once said "We find out by trial what is best and when we have found a good thing we stick to it."

It is perhaps fair to say that their furniture was the forerunner of our present day functional furniture.

On all candlestands, sewing stands or other stands with a pedestal, the legs are dovetailed to the shaft and the grain should run as nearly parallel to the general direction of the leg as possible; a thin metal plate should be fastened to the underside of the shaft and extend about three quarters of an inch along the base of each leg, with a screw or nail put in the leg to keep them from spreading.

The first furniture made by the Shakers was usually given a coat of paint, such as dark red for the furniture in the workshops. Later the paint was thinned or stain was used, often so thin that the grain of the wood was visible. Also used was a light umber or raw sienna stain giving the furniture a light brown color. Some pieces were left with a natural finish, then a final coat of oil or varnish was applied. Beds were painted green, almost bottle green, but shades varied.

So far I have only mentioned furniture, but under the heading of "Woodenware," the Shakers made hundreds of very beautiful and interesting items such as oval boxes, sewing boxes, carriers, trays, dippers, cups, scoops, candle and cutlery boxes, berry boxes and hundreds of specially designed tools and gadgets for the use of both the Sisters and Brethren in their workshops and kitchens. Some of the woodenware and other items were made to sell from their salesrooms to the outside world such as the beautiful oval boxes and sewing boxes. The oval boxes and carriers were usually made of maple. The bottoms and covers were fitted with quarter-sawn edge-grained pine. First the "fingers" or "lappers" are cut on the maple bands, then steamed and wrapped around an oval form, then the fingers are fastened with small copper or iron rivets (tacks) after they are dry and sanded. The pine disks are fitted into the bottom and cover and fastened with small square copper or iron brads.

When making a reproduction, I believe you must copy exactly every detail of the original, and use the same kind of wood and finish, because if you change such things as dimensions or profiles of mouldings, or cut-outs, then you are not making a true reproduction, but only a Shaker type piece of furniture.

Although I firmly believe than *no one* can make an "Antique" you should always mark your copy somewhere on the back or the bottom with your name and date in a way that it can not be erased. Please do not make any attempt to give it distress marks.

All this is not to say that it is wrong to make changes or design your own, but you are then making only a Shaker type piece of furniture. As a matter of fact, I have made for myself a secretary or what the Shakers properly would have called an upright desk, which follows very closely the design of two original Shaker pieces. The bottom section is a chest of drawers and the top section is a fall-front desk with place for papers and books, two small drawers, and above are two shelves with two doors (see pages number 76, 77). I never try to call it anything but a Shaker type of desk.

Whether you prefer to copy an original Shaker piece or design your own, I think it most important to carefully select the right kind of wood for the different projects, and be sure it is properly dried before using it. Another important rule is to follow good Shaker design and proportions. This applies to any kind of furniture, because without that, neither good materials nor the best of workmanship will produce good results. Finally you should never start anything before having made a detailed and measured drawing of the piece of furniture or work in mind.

I hope that these drawings will be helpful to craftsmen and collectors alike.

E.H.

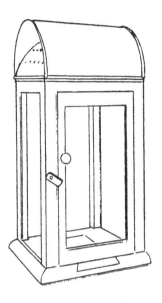

"ALL BEAUTY THAT HAS NOT
A FOUNDATION IN USE SOON
GROWS DISTASTEFUL AND NEEDS
CONTINUAL REPLACEMENT"

PIE-SAFE
WITH PIERCED TIN PANELS
SOUTH UNION, KENTUCKY

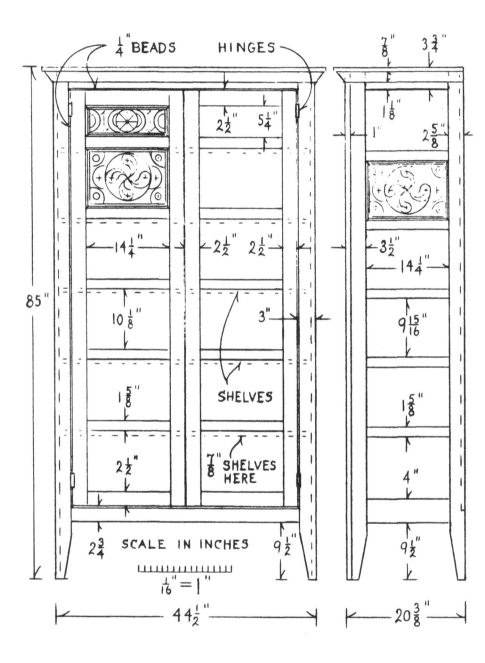

$\frac{1}{4}''$ BEADS   HINGES

$2\frac{1}{2}''$ $5\frac{1}{4}''$

$\frac{7}{8}''$ $3\frac{3}{4}''$

$1\frac{1}{8}''$

$1''$ $2\frac{5}{8}''$

$14\frac{1}{4}''$ $2\frac{1}{2}''$ $2\frac{1}{2}''$

$3\frac{1}{2}''$

$14\frac{1}{4}''$

$85''$

$10\frac{1}{8}''$ $3''$

$9\frac{15}{16}''$

$1\frac{5}{8}''$ SHELVES $1\frac{5}{8}''$

$2\frac{1}{2}''$ $\frac{7}{8}''$ SHELVES HERE $4''$

$2\frac{3}{4}''$ SCALE IN INCHES $9\frac{1}{2}''$ $9\frac{1}{2}''$

$\frac{1}{16}'' = 1''$

$44\frac{1}{2}''$ $20\frac{3}{8}''$

2

PIERCED TIN PANELS FOR PIE-SAFE
PIERCED TOWARD THE OUTSIDE
TO HELP KEEP INSECTS OUT
SOUTH UNION, KENTUCKY

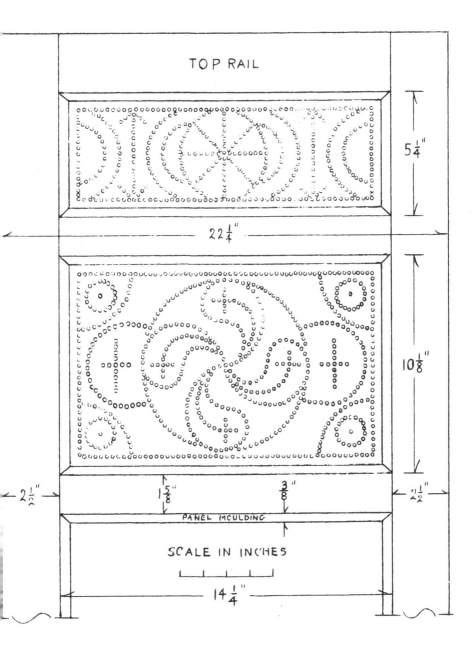

TOP RAIL

$5\frac{1}{4}''$

$22\frac{1}{4}''$

$10\frac{1}{8}''$

$2\frac{1}{2}''$ $1\frac{5}{8}''$ $\frac{3}{8}''$ $2\frac{1}{2}''$

PANEL MOULDING

SCALE IN INCHES

$14\frac{1}{4}''$

PINE CUPBOARD CHEST

ANDREWS COLLECTION

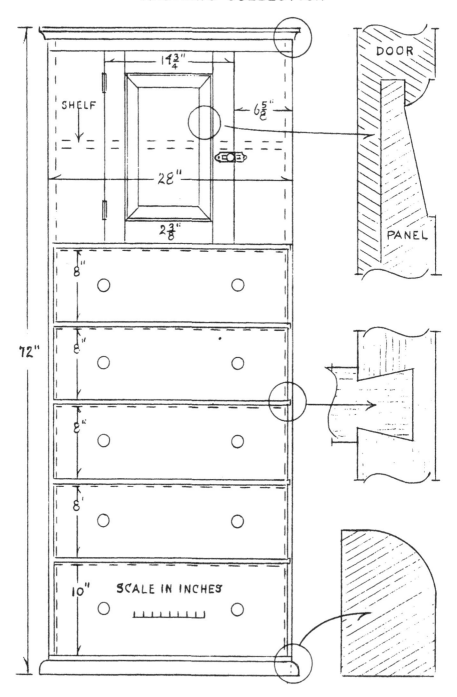

DOOR

PANEL

SHELF

$14\frac{3}{4}$"

$6\frac{5}{8}$"

28"

$2\frac{3}{8}$"

72"

8"

8"

8"

8'

10"

SCALE IN INCHES

PINE CUPBOARD CHEST
LIGHT-BROWN STAIN AND VARNISH
ANDREWS COLLECTION

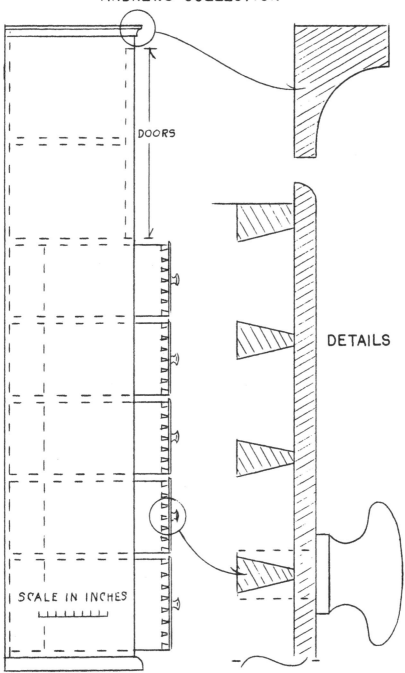

DOORS

DETAILS

SCALE IN INCHES

SILL CUPBOARD
FROM WATERVLIET COMMUNITY
PINE, STAINED LIGHT BROWN

FROM ANDREWS COLLECTION

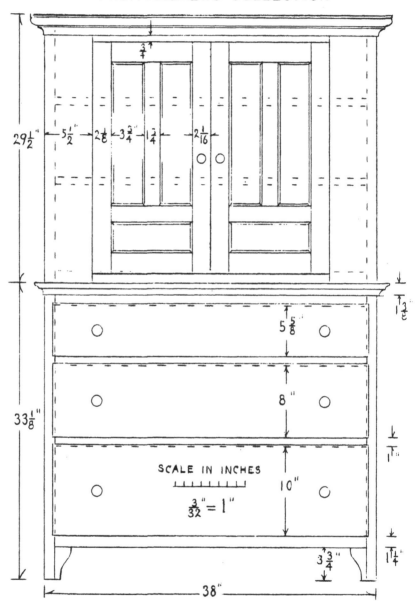

SCALE IN INCHES

$\frac{3}{32}'' = 1''$

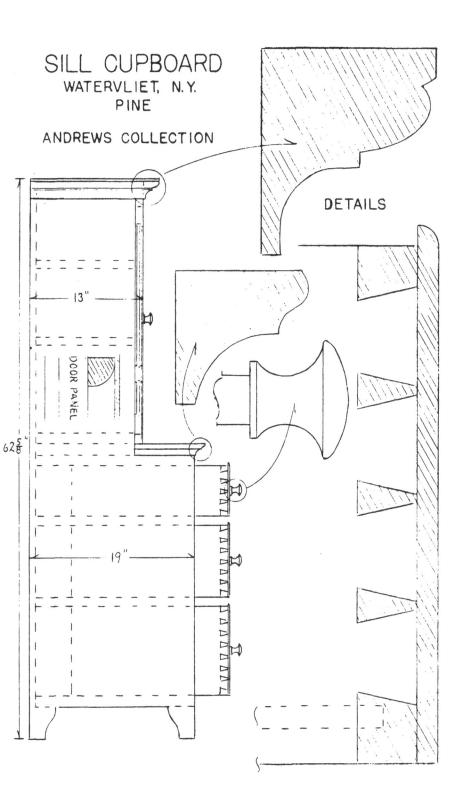

SILL CUPBOARD
WATERVLIET, N.Y.
PINE

ANDREWS COLLECTION

DETAILS

13"

DOOR PANEL

$62\frac{5}{8}$"

19"

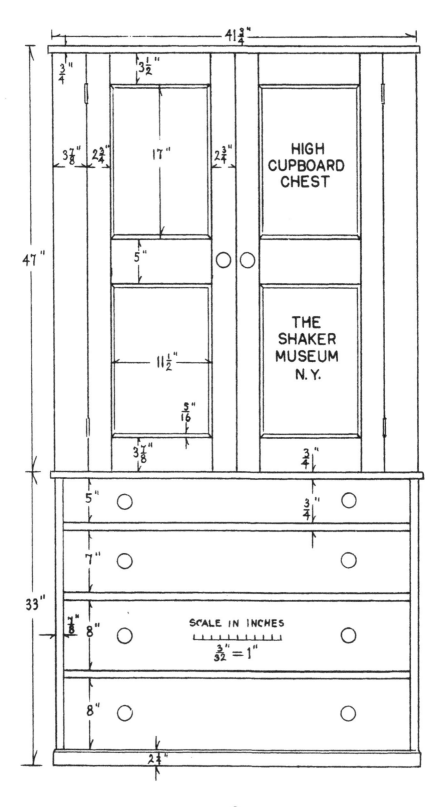

HIGH
CUPBOARD
CHEST

THE
SHAKER
MUSEUM
N.Y.

SCALE IN INCHES

$\frac{3}{32}$" = 1"

8

HIGH CUPBOARD ON CHEST

THE SHAKER MUSEUM
OLD CHATHAM, N.Y.

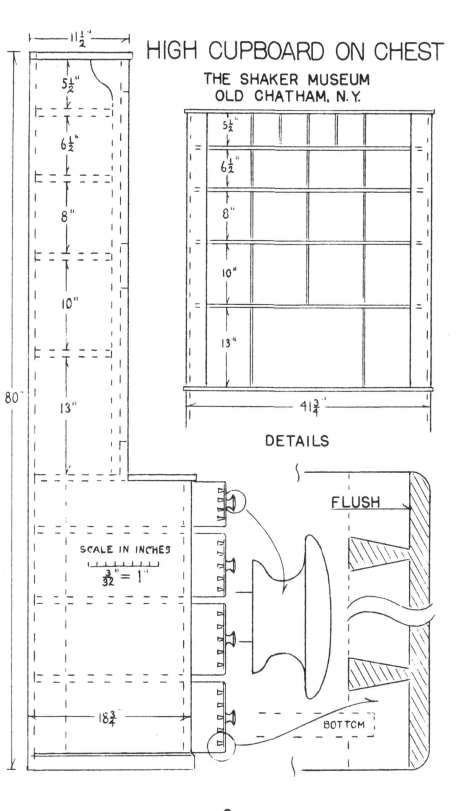

DETAILS

FLUSH

SCALE IN INCHES

$\frac{3}{32}'' = 1''$

BOTTOM

HIGH CUPBOARD CHEST

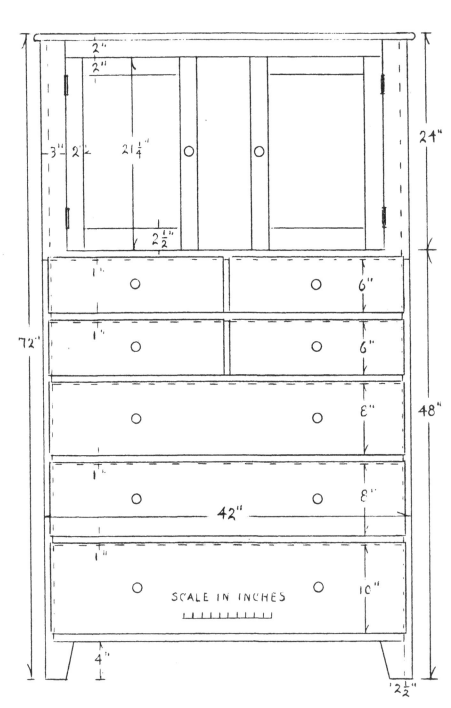

SCALE IN INCHES

10

CUPBOARD CHEST

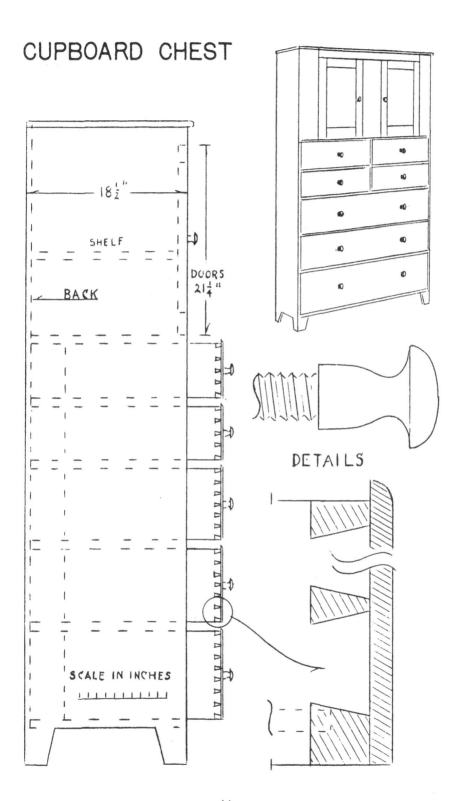

18½"

SHELF

DOORS
21¼"

BACK

SCALE IN INCHES

DETAILS

HIGH CUPBOARD CHEST
THE SHAKER MUSEUM, OLD CHATHAM, N.Y.

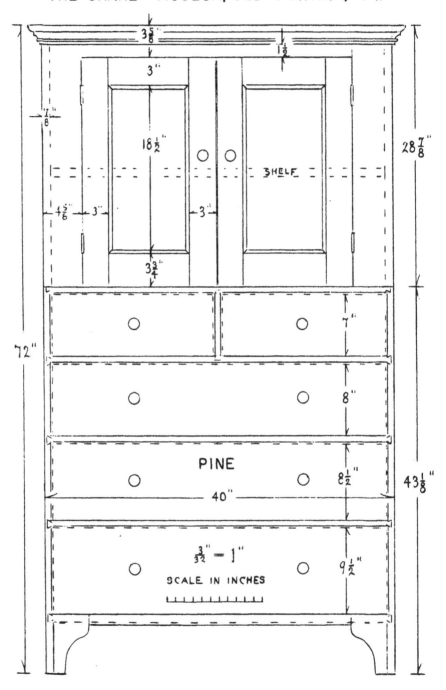

HIGH CUPBOARD CHEST
THE SHAKER MUSEUM, OLD CHATHAM, N.Y.

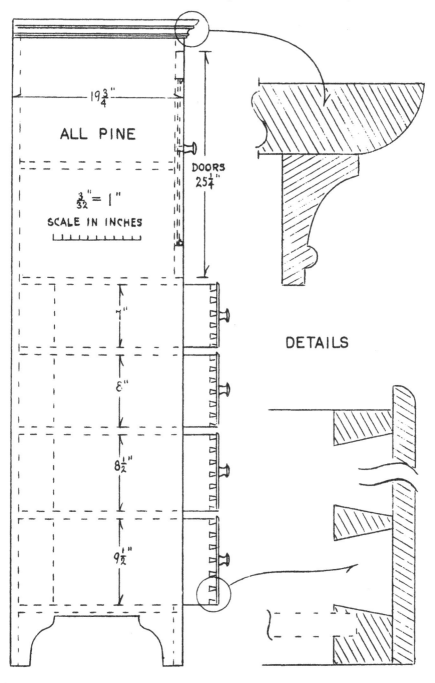

ALL PINE

$19\frac{3}{4}''$

DOORS $25\frac{1}{4}''$

$\frac{3}{32}'' = 1''$

SCALE IN INCHES

$7''$

$8''$

$8\frac{1}{2}''$

$9\frac{1}{2}''$

DETAILS

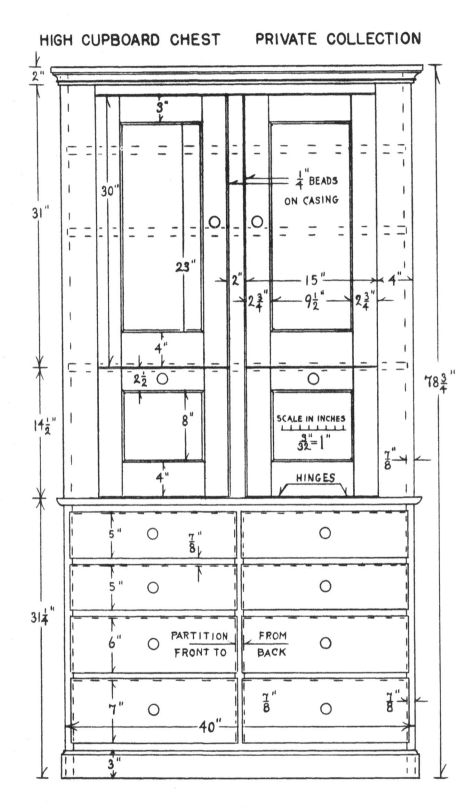

HIGH CUPBOARD CHEST

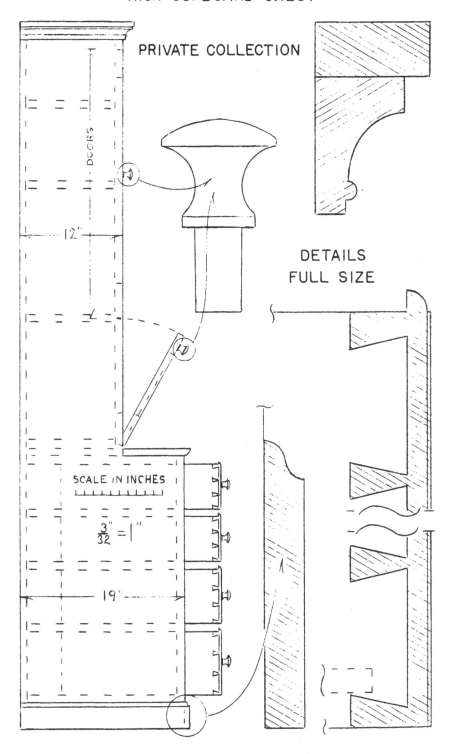

PRIVATE COLLECTION

DOORS

12"

DETAILS
FULL SIZE

SCALE IN INCHES

$\frac{3"}{32} = 1"$

19"

PINE CUPBOARD CHEST
LIGHT-BROWN STAIN AND VARNISH

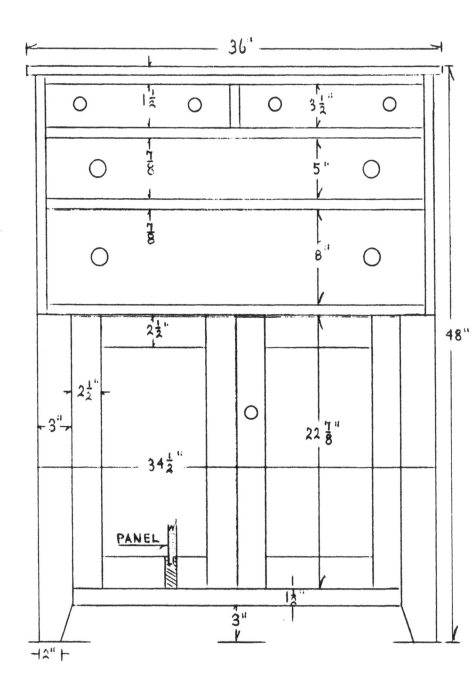

PINE CUPBOARD CHEST
LIGHT-BROWN STAIN AND VARNISH

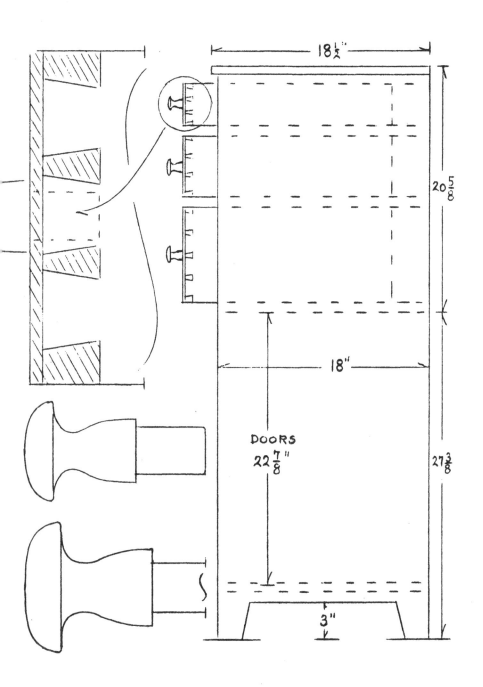

TAILORESSES' SHOP COUNTER

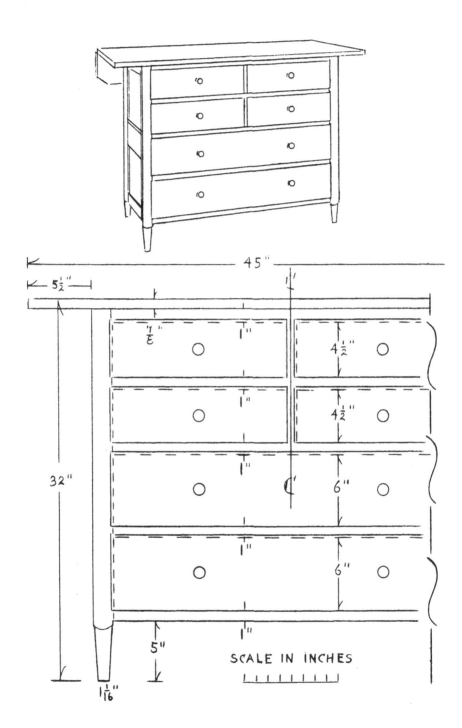

45"

5½"

1"

7/8"

1"

4½"

1"

4½"

32"

1"

6"

1"

6"

1"

5"

SCALE IN INCHES

1 1/16"

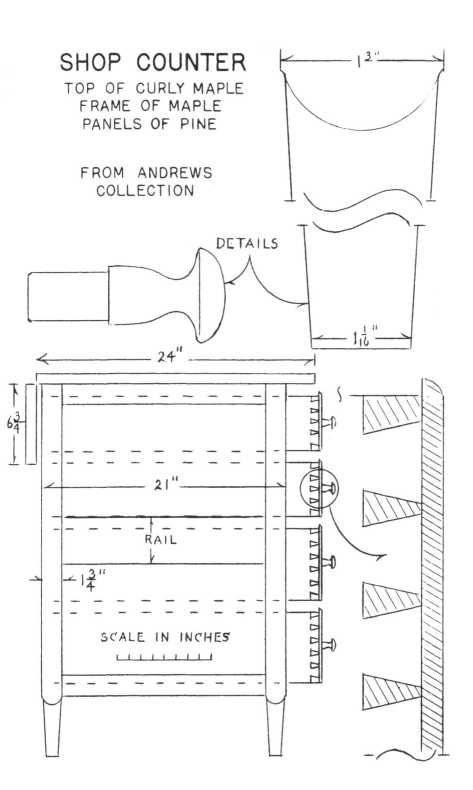

SHOP COUNTER
TOP OF CURLY MAPLE
FRAME OF MAPLE
PANELS OF PINE

FROM ANDREWS
COLLECTION

$1\frac{3}{4}$"

DETAILS

$1\frac{1}{16}$"

24"

$6\frac{3}{4}$

21"

RAIL

$1\frac{3}{4}$"

SCALE IN INCHES

TAILORING COUNTER

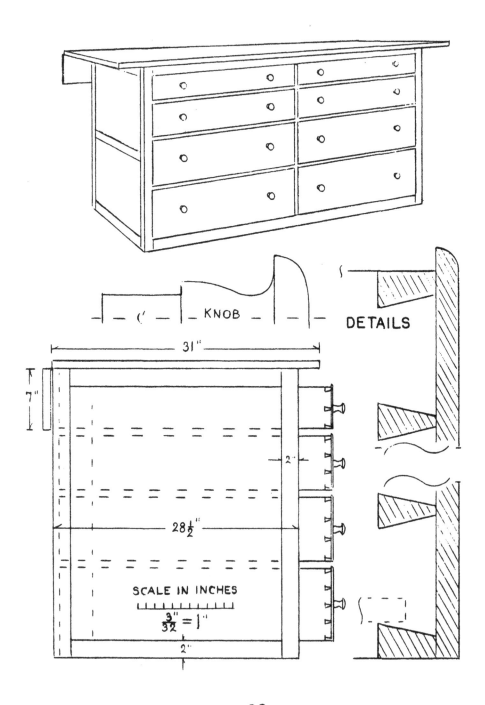

KNOB

DETAILS

31"

7"

28½"

2"

SCALE IN INCHES

$\frac{3"}{32} = 1"$

2"

TAILORING COUNTER
A COMBINATION OF TABLE
AND CHEST OF DRAWERS

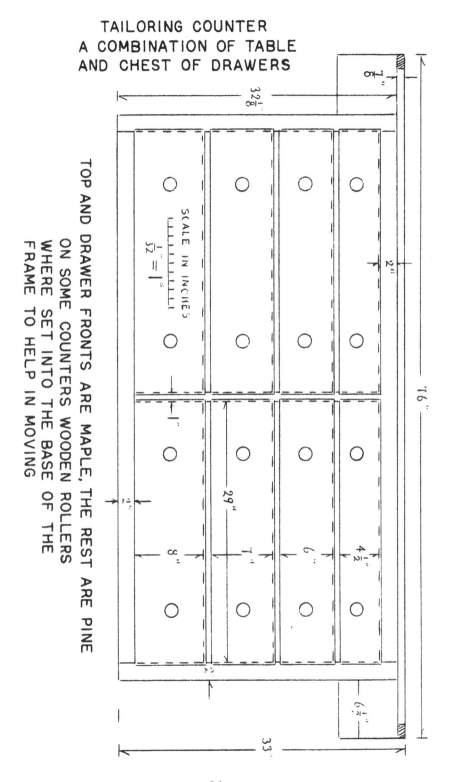

TOP AND DRAWER FRONTS ARE MAPLE, THE REST ARE PINE
ON SOME COUNTERS WOODEN ROLLERS
WHERE SET INTO THE BASE OF THE
FRAME TO HELP IN MOVING

SCALE IN INCHES

$\frac{1}{32} = 1"$

STORAGE BENCH ca. 1800

THE SHAKER MUSEUM, OLD CHATHAM, N.Y.

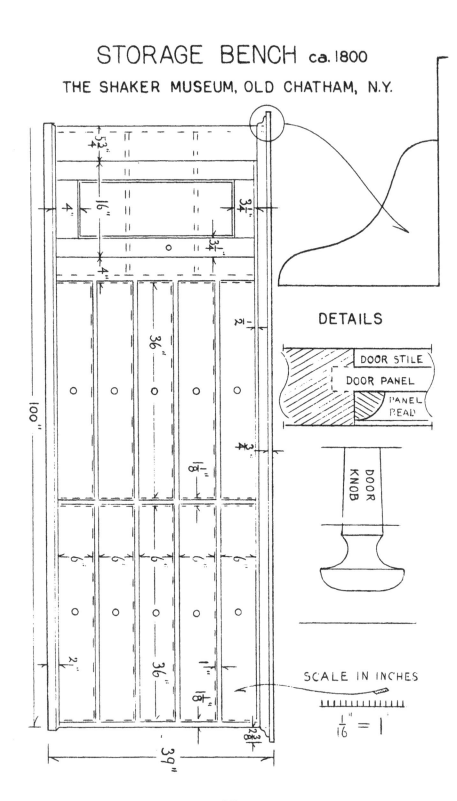

DETAILS

DOOR STILE

DOOR PANEL

PANEL BEAD

DOOR KNOB

SCALE IN INCHES

$\frac{1}{16}'' = 1$

STORAGE BENCH ca. 1800
PINE, PAINTED BLUE
FROM CANTERBURY, N. H.

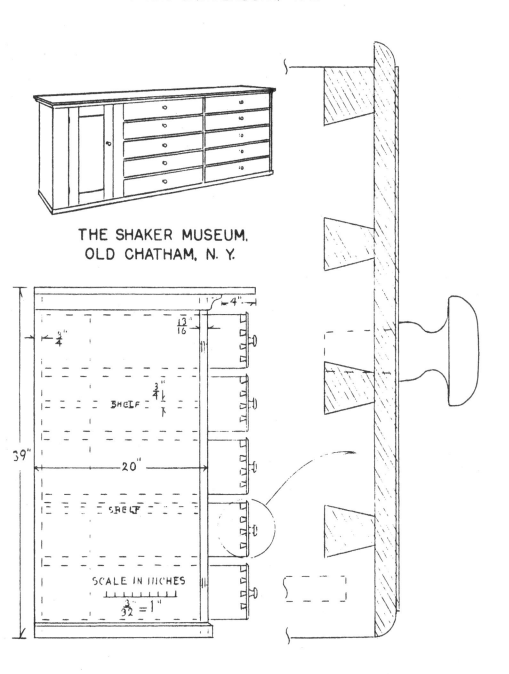

THE SHAKER MUSEUM,
OLD CHATHAM, N. Y.

SHELF

SHELF

39"

4"

13/16

3/4"

3/4"

20"

SCALE IN INCHES

3/32 = 1"

CHEST OF DRAWERS
FROM NEW LEBANON

GREEN WILLOW FARM, CHATHAM N.Y.

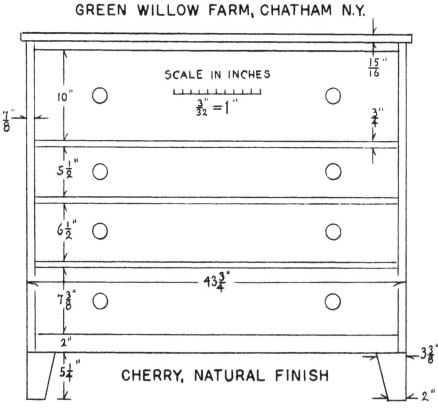

SCALE IN INCHES

$\frac{3}{32}" = 1"$

CHERRY, NATURAL FINISH

24

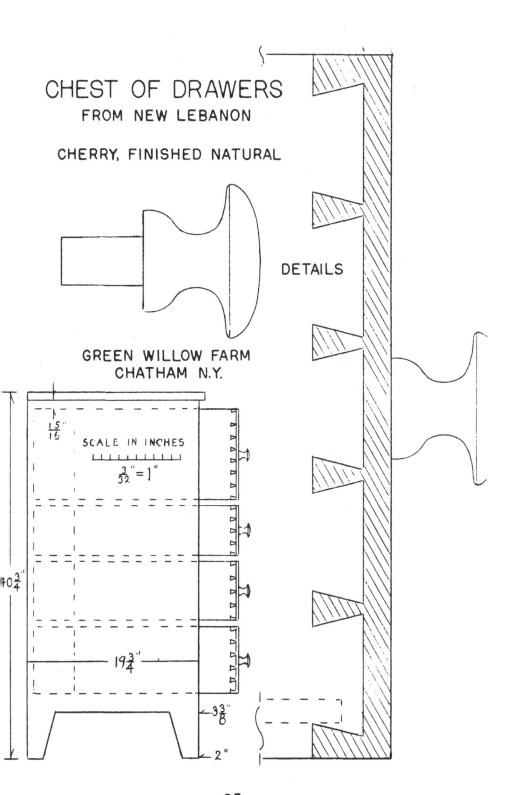

CHEST OF DRAWERS
FROM NEW LEBANON

CHERRY, FINISHED NATURAL

DETAILS

GREEN WILLOW FARM
CHATHAM N.Y.

SCALE IN INCHES

$\frac{3}{32}" = 1"$

$\frac{15}{16}"$

$40\frac{3}{4}"$

$19\frac{3}{4}"$

$3\frac{3}{8}"$

$2"$

CHEST
OF
DRAWERS
FROM NEW LEBANON

PRIVATE COLLECTION

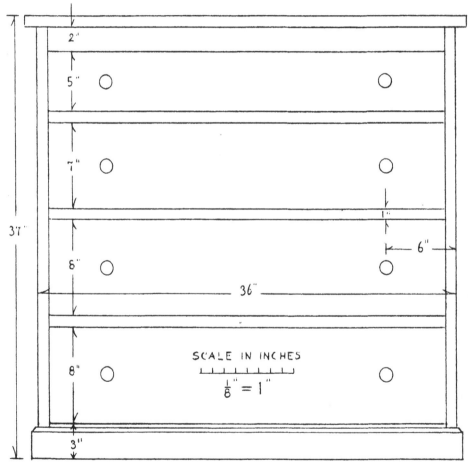

SCALE IN INCHES

$\frac{1}{8}" = 1"$

CHEST of DRAWERS
FROM NEW LEBANON
CHERRY AND PINE

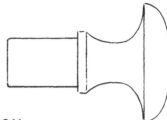

PRIVATE COLLECTION

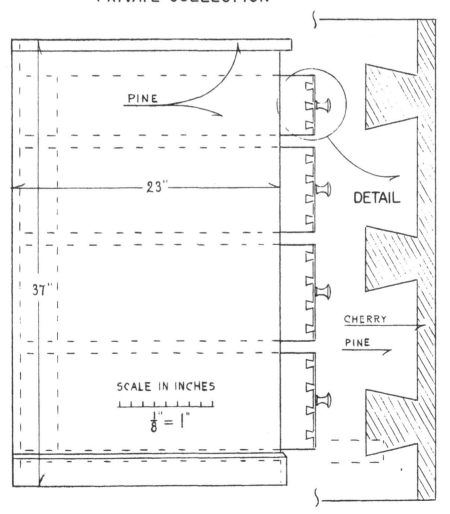

PINE

23"

37"

DETAIL

CHERRY

PINE

SCALE IN INCHES

$\frac{1}{8}" = 1"$

SMALL CASE OF DRAWERS — BUTTERNUT
FROM ENFIELD CONN. 1849

BOSTON MUSEUM OF FINE ARTS, BOSTON MASS.

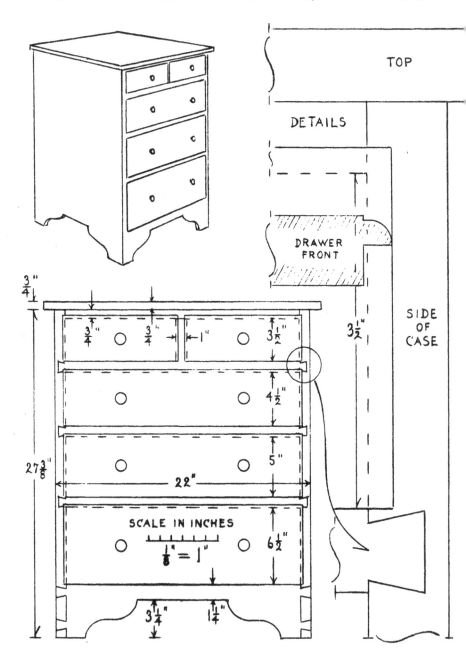

TOP

DETAILS

DRAWER FRONT

SIDE OF CASE

$3\frac{1}{2}$

$\frac{3}{4}''$

$\frac{3}{4}''$

$\frac{3}{4}''$

$1''$

$3\frac{1}{2}''$

$4\frac{1}{2}''$

$5''$

$22''$

$27\frac{3}{8}''$

$6\frac{1}{2}''$

SCALE IN INCHES

$\frac{1}{8}'' = 1''$

$3\frac{1}{4}''$

$1\frac{1}{4}''$

CASE OF DRAWERS — BUTTERNUT
FROM ENFIELD CONN. 1849

BOSTON MUSEUM OF FINE ARTS, BOSTON MASS.

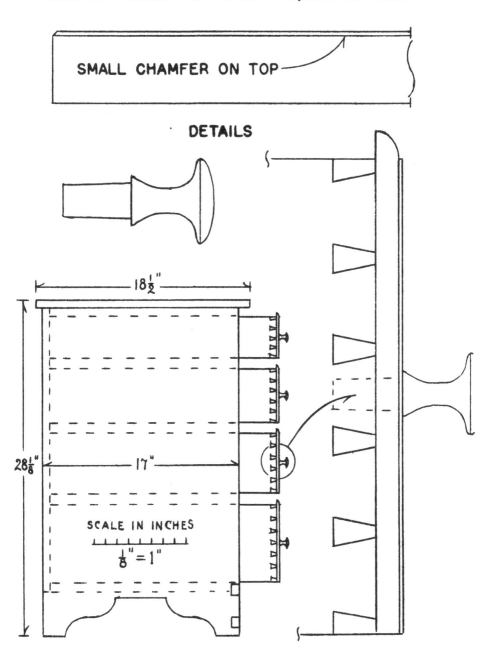

SMALL CHAMFER ON TOP

DETAILS

$18\frac{1}{2}''$

$28\frac{1}{8}''$

$17''$

SCALE IN INCHES

$\frac{1}{8}'' = 1''$

SHAKER UPRIGHT DESK

MAPLE CASE – CHERRY LEGS

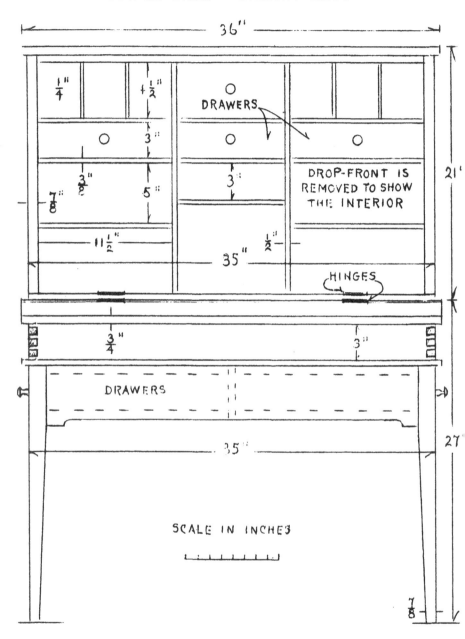

DRAWERS

DROP-FRONT IS
REMOVED TO SHOW
THE INTERIOR

HINGES

DRAWERS

SCALE IN INCHES

SHAKER UPRIGHT DESK
MAPLE CASE — CHERRY LEGS

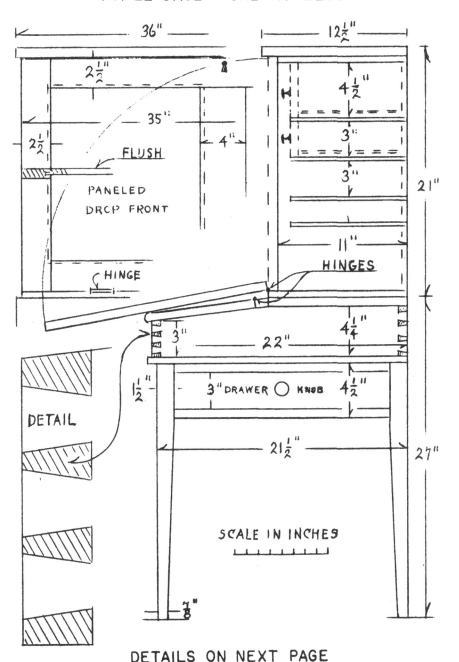

36"   12½"

2½"

35"

4½"

FLUSH

2½"   4"   3"

PANELED
DROP FRONT   3"

21"

11"

HINGE   HINGES

3"   4¼"

DETAIL   22"

1½"   3" DRAWER ○ KNOB   4½"

21½"   27"

SCALE IN INCHES

⅞"

DETAILS ON NEXT PAGE

31

DETAILS OF UPRIGHT DESK

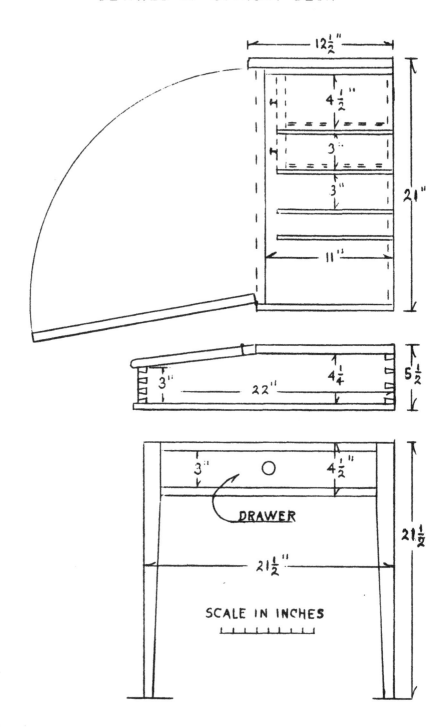

SCALE IN INCHES

DETAILS OF UPRIGHT DESK

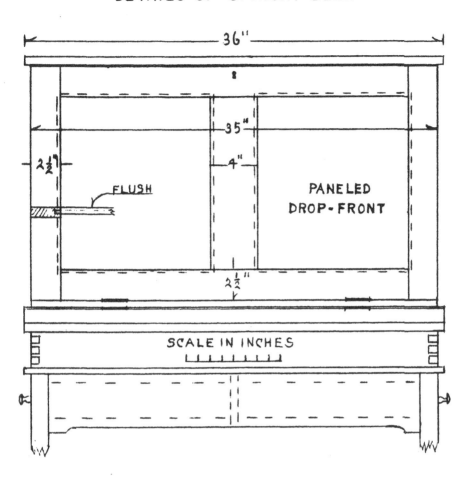

FLUSH

PANELED
DROP-FRONT

SCALE IN INCHES

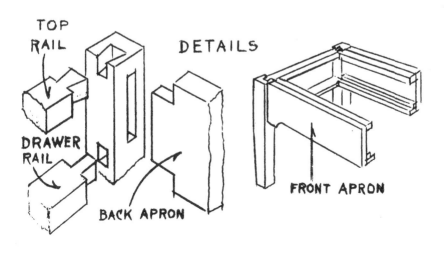

TOP
RAIL

DETAILS

DRAWER
RAIL

BACK APRON

FRONT APRON

33

SCHOOL DESK

OAK AND CHERRY

$\frac{1}{8}" = 1"$

SCALE IN INCHES

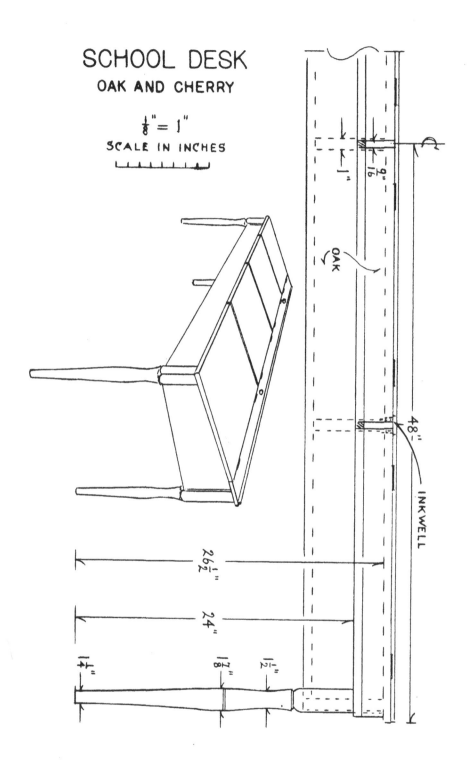

SCHOOL DESK

OAK AND CHERRY
FROM ANDREWS COLLECTION

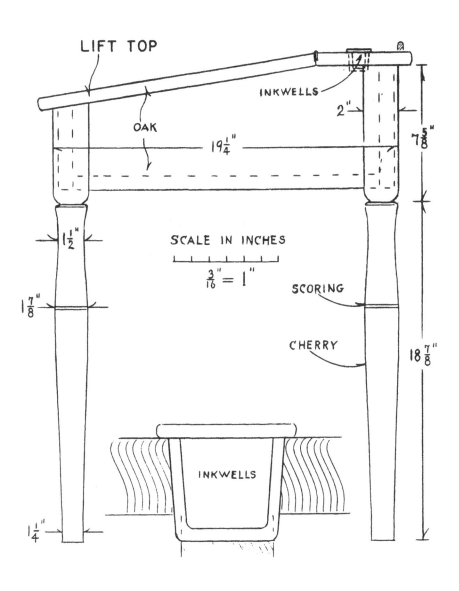

LIFT TOP

INKWELLS

OAK

$19\frac{1}{4}$"

2"

$7\frac{5}{8}$"

$1\frac{1}{2}$"

SCALE IN INCHES

$\frac{3}{16}$" = 1"

SCORING

CHERRY

$1\frac{7}{8}$"

$18\frac{7}{8}$"

INKWELLS

$1\frac{1}{4}$"

TABLE DESK
FROM CANTERBURY N.H.

ALL
PINE

PAINTED
YELLOW

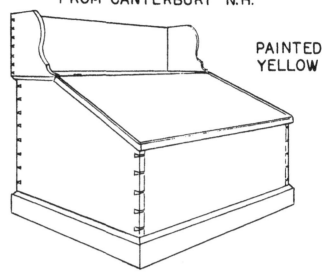

GREEN WILLOW FARM, CHATHAM N.Y.

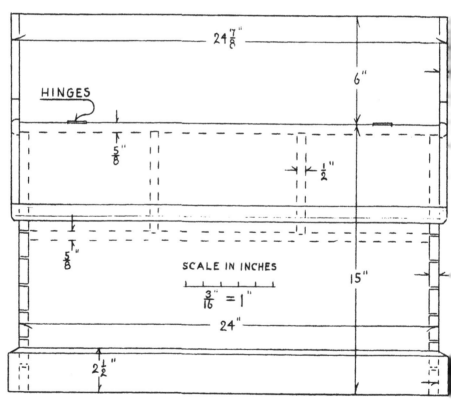

24⅞"

6"

HINGES

5/8"

½"

5/8"

SCALE IN INCHES

3/16" = 1"

24"

15"

2½"

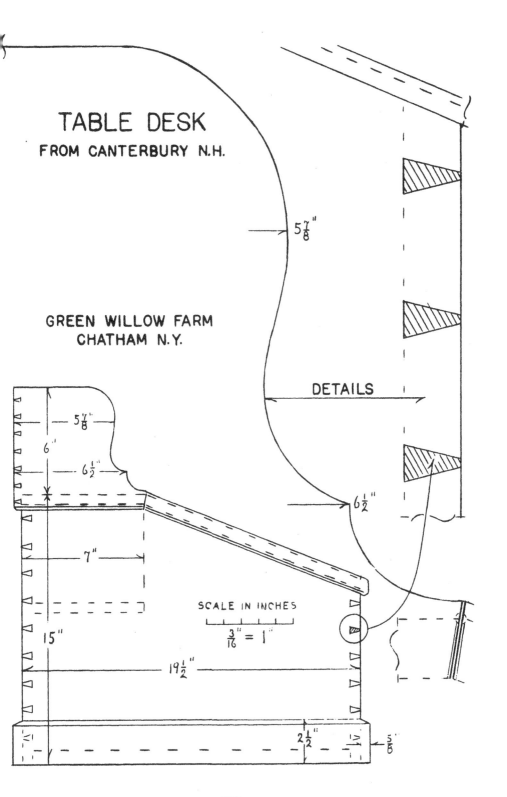

TABLE DESK
FROM CANTERBURY N.H.

GREEN WILLOW FARM
CHATHAM N.Y.

DETAILS

$5\frac{7}{8}$"

$6\frac{1}{2}$"

$5\frac{7}{8}$"

6"

$6\frac{1}{2}$"

7"

15"

SCALE IN INCHES
$\frac{3}{16}$" = 1"

$19\frac{1}{2}$"

$2\frac{1}{2}$"

$\frac{5}{8}$"

PINE SEWING STAND

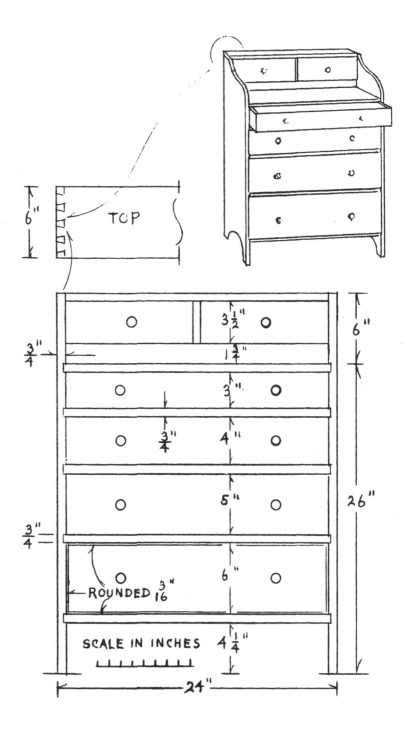

TOP

6"

3½"

1¾"

3".

¾"

4"

5"

6"

6"

26"

¾"

¾"

ROUNDED 3/16"

SCALE IN INCHES   4¼"

24"

PINE SEWING STAND
LIGHT-BROWN STAIN AND VARNISH

WRITING OR CUTTING BOARD SET IN TOP
OF LONG DRAWER, REMOVABLE AT WILL

ALL DRAWERS
RABBETED AND NAILED

CORNERS ROUNDED $\frac{3}{16}$"

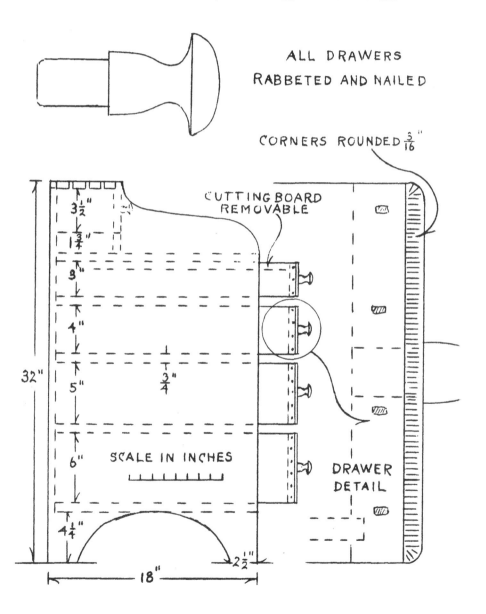

CUTTING BOARD
REMOVABLE

$3\frac{1}{2}$"

$1\frac{3}{4}$"

3"

4"

5"

$\frac{3}{4}$"

6"

SCALE IN INCHES

32"

$4\frac{1}{4}$"

$2\frac{1}{2}$"

18"

DRAWER
DETAIL

SEWING TABLE

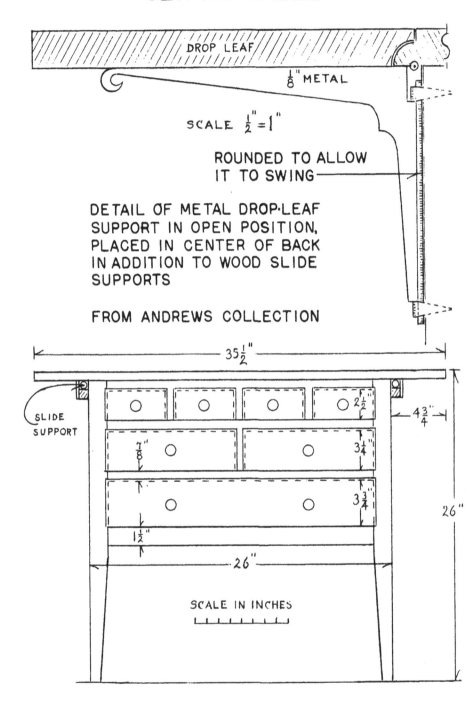

DROP LEAF

$\frac{1}{8}$" METAL

SCALE $\frac{1}{2}$" = 1"

ROUNDED TO ALLOW
IT TO SWING

DETAIL OF METAL DROP-LEAF
SUPPORT IN OPEN POSITION,
PLACED IN CENTER OF BACK
IN ADDITION TO WOOD SLIDE
SUPPORTS

FROM ANDREWS COLLECTION

$35\frac{1}{2}$"

SLIDE
SUPPORT

$2\frac{1}{2}$"

$4\frac{3}{4}$"

$\frac{7}{8}$"

$3\frac{1}{4}$"

$3\frac{3}{4}$"

26"

$1\frac{1}{2}$"

26"

SCALE IN INCHES

SEWING TABLE
CHERRY TOP AND FRAME PINE PANELS
ANDREWS COLLECTION

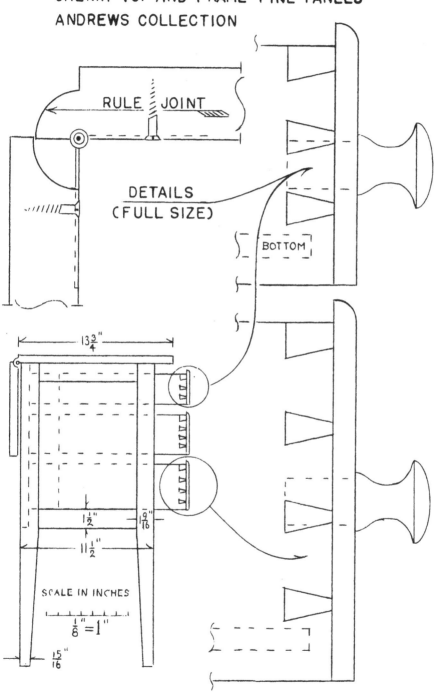

RULE JOINT

DETAILS
(FULL SIZE)

BOTTOM

$13\frac{3}{4}"$

$1\frac{1}{2}"$ $\frac{9}{16}"$

$11\frac{1}{2}"$

SCALE IN INCHES

$\frac{1}{8}"=1"$

$\frac{15}{16}"$

SEWING TABLE
TOP SECTION PROBABLY ADDED LATER

FROM NEW LEBANON   PRIVATE COLLECTION

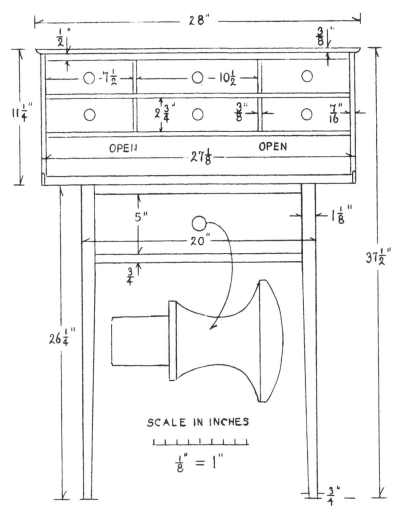

SCALE IN INCHES

$\frac{1}{8}'' = 1''$

ALL DRAWER FRONTS AND TABLE LEGS ARE CHERRY

SEWING TABLE
FROM NEW LEBANON

CHERRY, MAPLE
AND CHESTNUT

PRIVATE COLLECTION

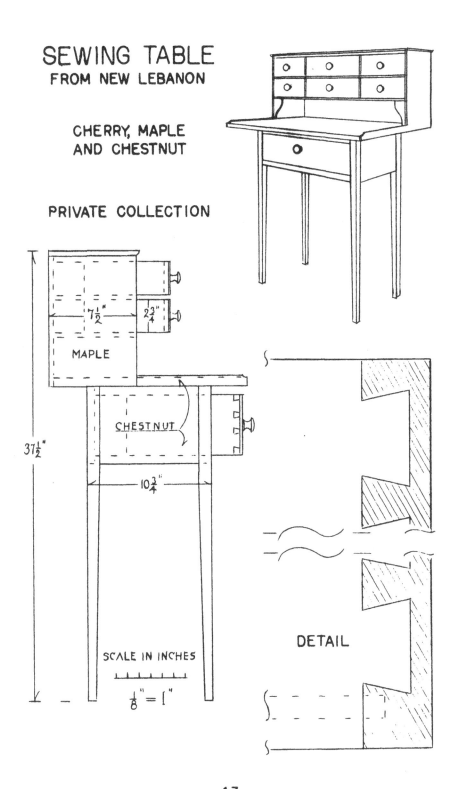

MAPLE

$7\frac{1}{2}$" $2\frac{3}{4}$"

CHESTNUT

$37\frac{1}{2}$"

$10\frac{3}{4}$"

SCALE IN INCHES

$\frac{1}{8}$" = 1"

DETAIL

43

SEWING TABLE
MADE OF BUTTERNUT

PRIVATE COLLECTION

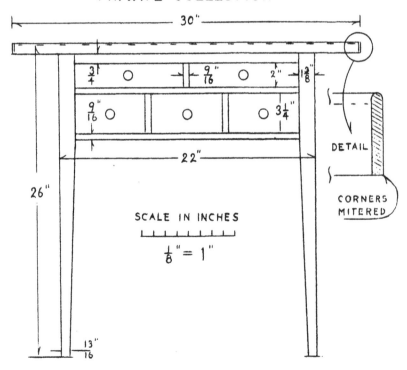

SCALE IN INCHES

$\frac{1}{8}" = 1"$

DETAIL

CORNERS MITERED

SEWING TABLE
MADE OF BUTTERNUT

PRIVATE COLLECTION

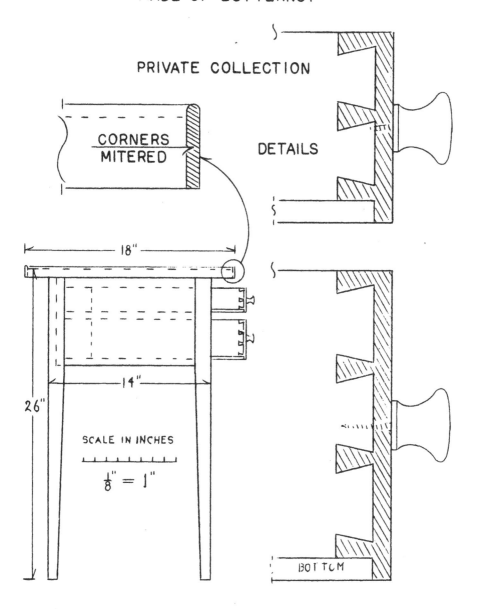

CORNERS MITERED

DETAILS

18"

14"

26"

SCALE IN INCHES

$\frac{1}{8}" = 1"$

BOTTOM

45

PINE WASH-STAND
NEW LEBANON N.Y.

MUSEUM OF FINE ARTS, BOSTON, MASS.

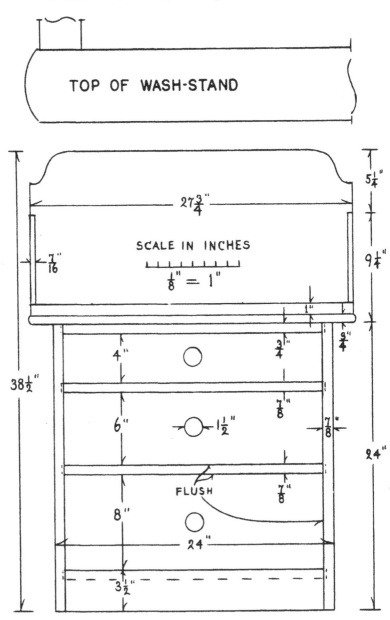

TOP OF WASH-STAND

SCALE IN INCHES

$\frac{1}{8}" = 1"$

FLUSH

PINE WASH-STAND
NEW LEBANON N.Y.

MUSEUM OF FINE ARTS, BOSTON, MASS.

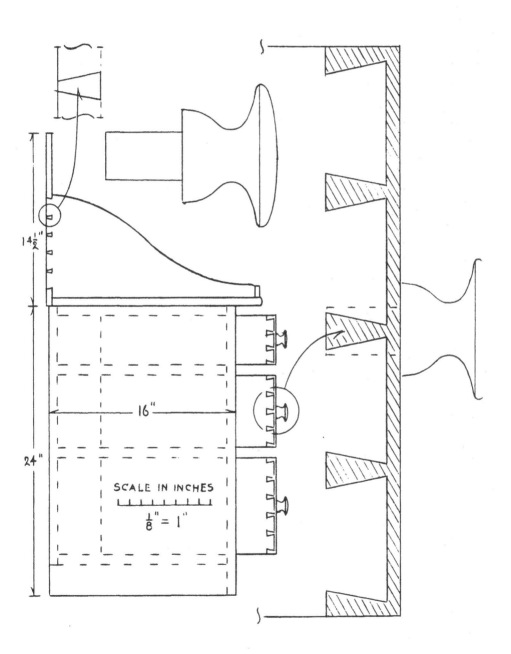

SCALE IN INCHES

$\frac{1}{8}" = 1"$

DINING TABLE
CANTERBURY, N.H.
BIRCH WITH TOP OF BUTTERNUT
THE SHAKER MUSEUM, OLD CHATHAM, N.Y.

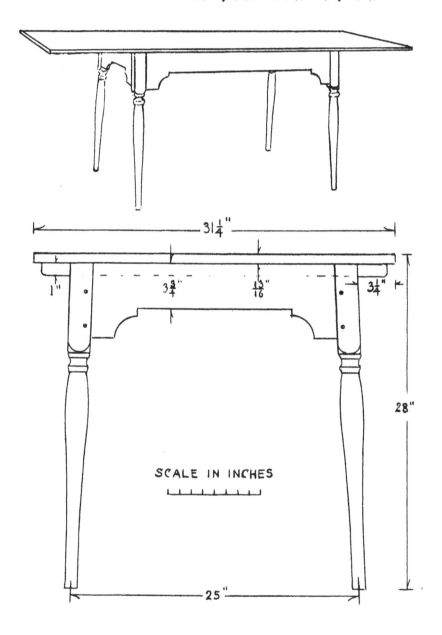

SCALE IN INCHES

48

DINING TABLE

CANTERBURY, N. H.

THE SHAKER MUSEUM, OLD CHATHAM, N.Y.

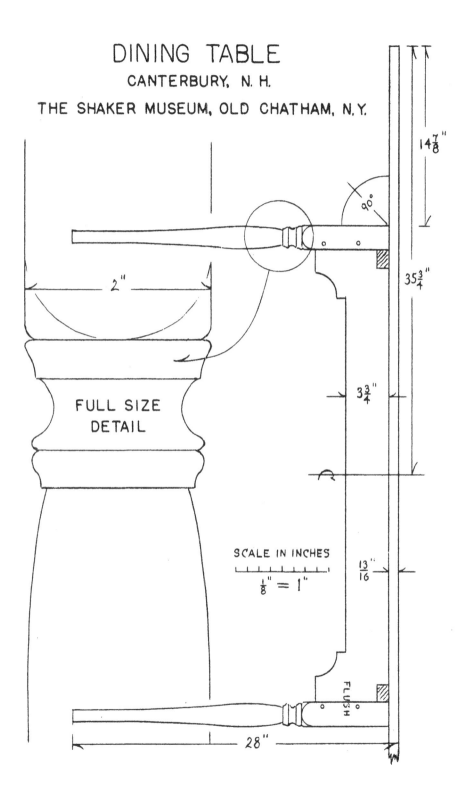

$14\frac{7}{8}"$

90°

$35\frac{3}{4}"$

2"

FULL SIZE
DETAIL

$3\frac{3}{4}"$

SCALE IN INCHES

$\frac{1}{8}" = 1"$

$\frac{13}{16}"$

FLUSH

28"

OVAL-TOP TABLE
BIRCH WITH PINE TOP

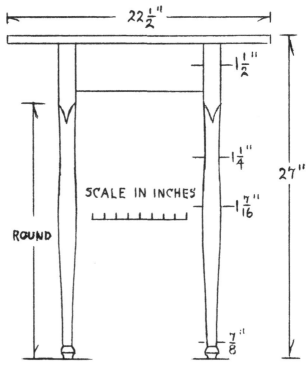

$22\frac{1}{2}''$

$1\frac{1}{2}''$

$1\frac{1}{4}''$

$1\frac{7}{16}''$

$27''$

SCALE IN INCHES

ROUND

$\frac{7}{8}''$

50

OVAL-TOP TABLE
BIRCH WITH PINE TOP

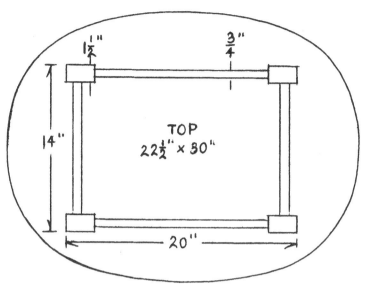

$1\frac{1}{2}$" $\frac{3}{4}$"

14"

TOP
$22\frac{1}{2}$" x 30"

20"

SCALE IN INCHES

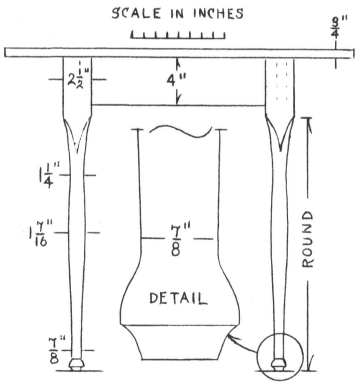

$\frac{3}{4}$"

$2\frac{1}{2}$" 4"

$1\frac{1}{4}$"

$1\frac{7}{16}$"

$\frac{7}{8}$"

$\frac{7}{8}$"

DETAIL

ROUND

ROUND PEDESTAL TABLE
DARROW SCHOOL, NEW LEBANON, N.Y.

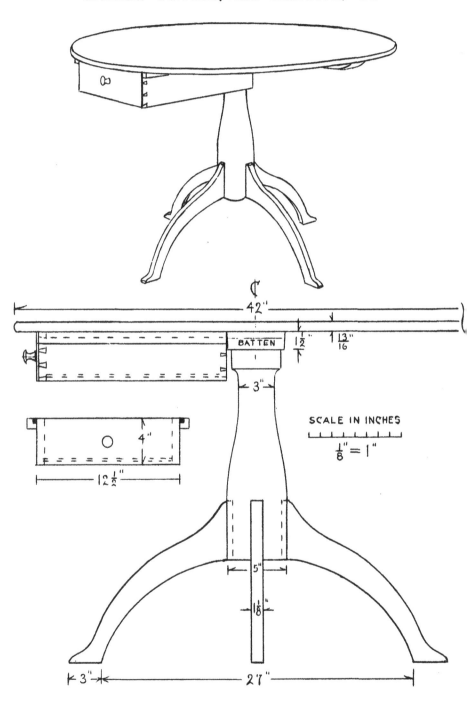

42"

BATTEN

1½"

1 13/16"

3"

4"

12½"

SCALE IN INCHES

⅛" = 1"

5"

1⅛"

3"

27"

PEDESTAL TABLE
DARROW SCHOOL, NEW LEBANON, N.Y.

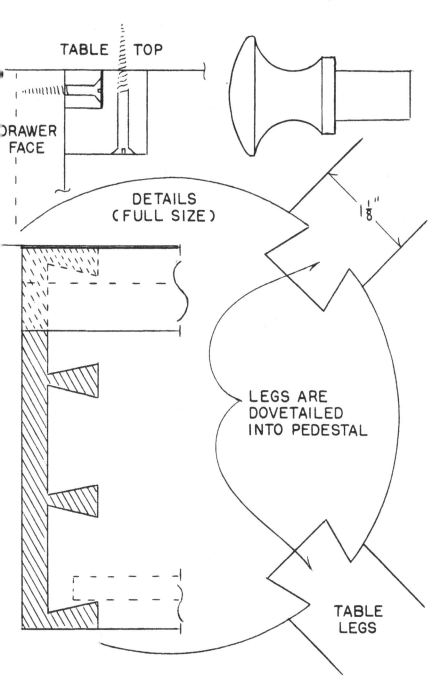

TABLE TOP

DRAWER FACE

DETAILS
(FULL SIZE)

$1\frac{1}{8}''$

LEGS ARE
DOVETAILED
INTO PEDESTAL

TABLE
LEGS

CANDLESTAND
PLEASANT HILL, KENTUCKY

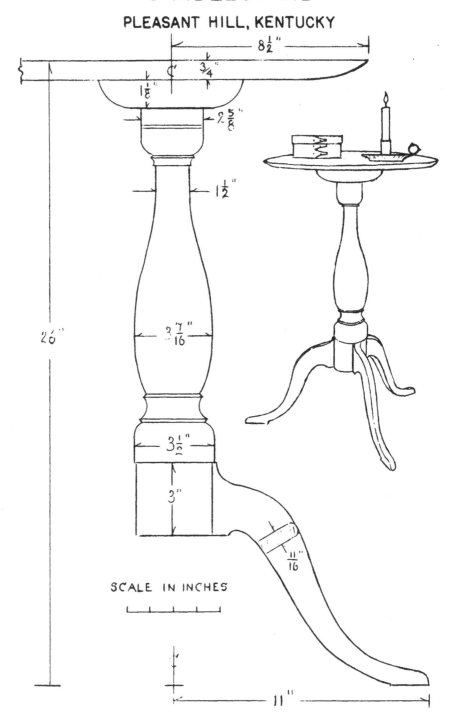

SCALE IN INCHES

54

CANDLESTAND
FROM MT. LEBANON

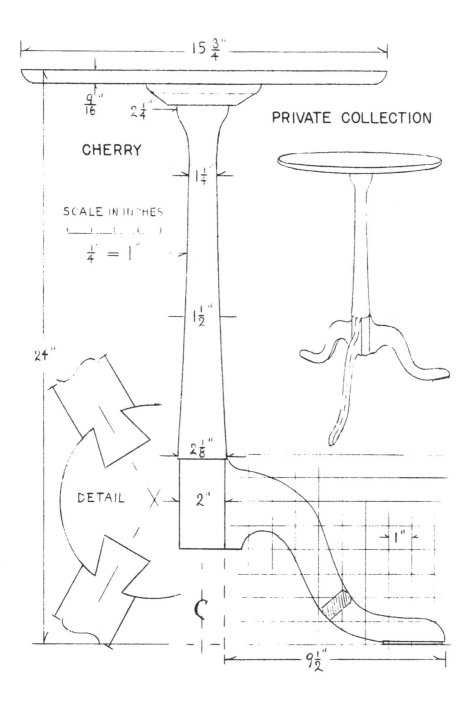

15 $\frac{3}{4}$"

PRIVATE COLLECTION

$\frac{9}{16}$"

2 $\frac{1}{4}$"

CHERRY

1 $\frac{1}{4}$"

SCALE IN INCHES

$\frac{1}{4}$ = 1"

1 $\frac{1}{2}$"

24"

2 $\frac{1}{8}$"

DETAIL   X

2"

1"

℃

9 $\frac{1}{2}$"

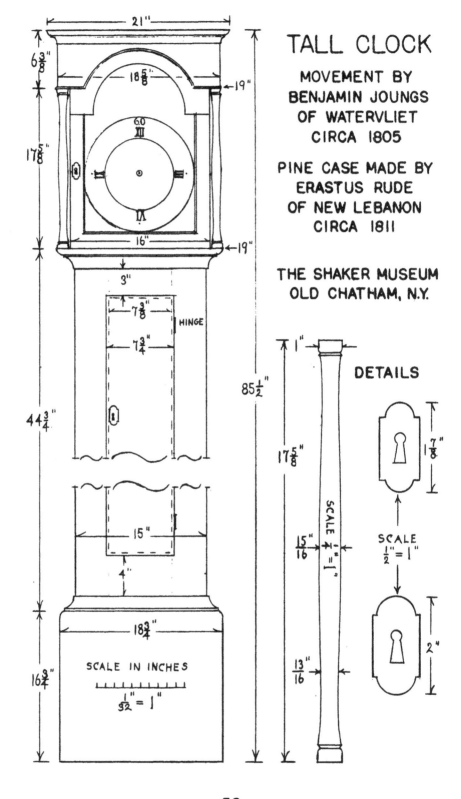

TALL CLOCK

MOVEMENT BY
BENJAMIN JOUNGS
OF WATERVLIET
CIRCA 1805

PINE CASE MADE BY
ERASTUS RUDE
OF NEW LEBANON
CIRCA 1811

THE SHAKER MUSEUM
OLD CHATHAM, N.Y.

DETAILS

SCALE
$\frac{1}{2}" = 1"$

SCALE $\frac{1}{4}" = 1"$

SCALE IN INCHES

$\frac{1}{32}" = 1"$

56

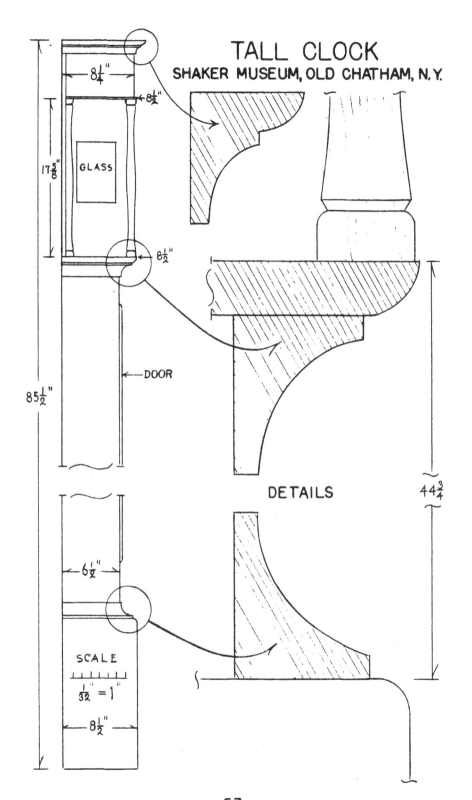

TALL CLOCK
SHAKER MUSEUM, OLD CHATHAM, N.Y.

$8\frac{1}{4}$"

$8\frac{1}{2}$"

$17\frac{5}{8}$"

GLASS

$8\frac{1}{2}$"

$85\frac{1}{2}$"

←DOOR

DETAILS

$44\frac{3}{4}$

$6\frac{1}{2}$"

SCALE

$\frac{1}{32}$" = 1"

$8\frac{1}{2}$"

PINE CASE OF SHAKER TALL CLOCK
FROM WATERVLIET

THE SHAKER MUSEUM, OLD CHATHAM, N.Y.

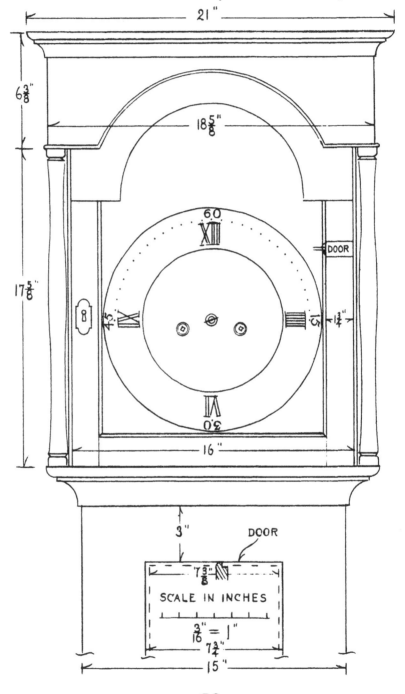

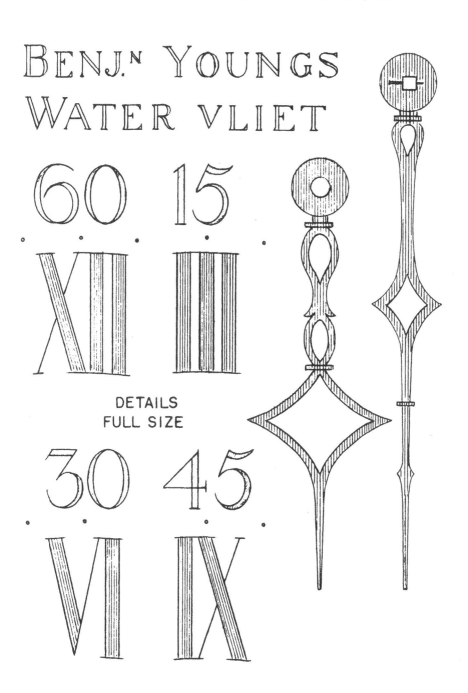

BENJ.ᴺ YOUNGS
WATER VLIET

60 15

XII III

DETAILS
FULL SIZE

30 45

VI IX

59

WOOD BOX
PLEASANT HILL, KENTUCKY

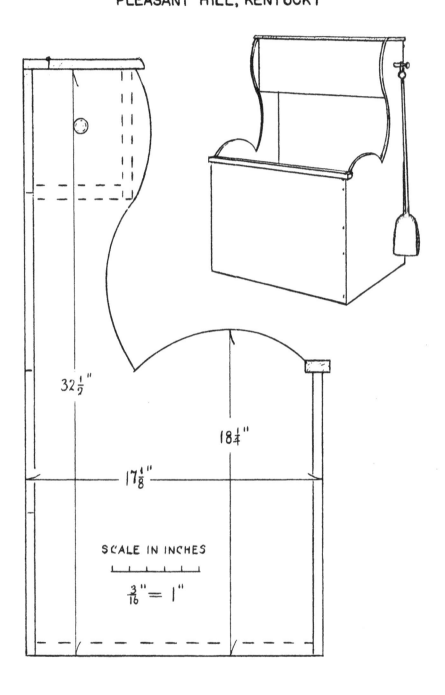

$32\frac{1}{2}''$

$18\frac{1}{4}''$

$17\frac{1}{8}''$

SCALE IN INCHES

$\frac{3}{16}'' = 1''$

WOOD BOX

PLEASANT HILL, KENTUCKY

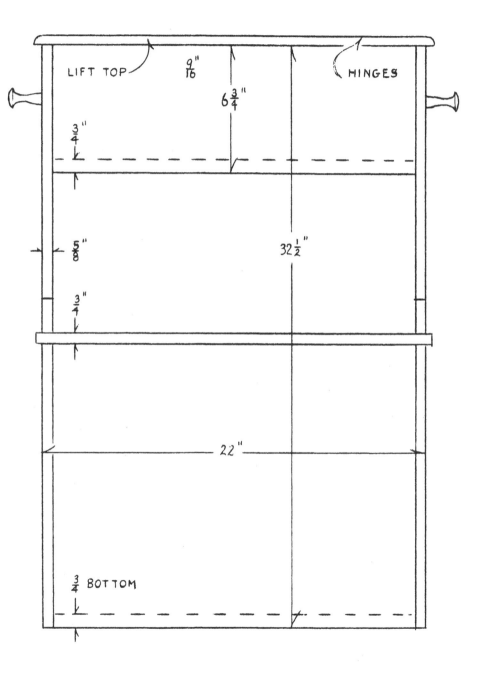

LIFT TOP

$\frac{9}{16}''$

HINGES

$6\frac{3}{4}''$

$\frac{3}{4}''$

$\frac{5}{8}''$

$32\frac{1}{2}''$

$\frac{3}{4}''$

$22''$

$\frac{3}{4}$ BOTTOM

CANTERBURY SETTEE
THE SHAKER MUSEUM   OLD CHATHAM, N. Y.

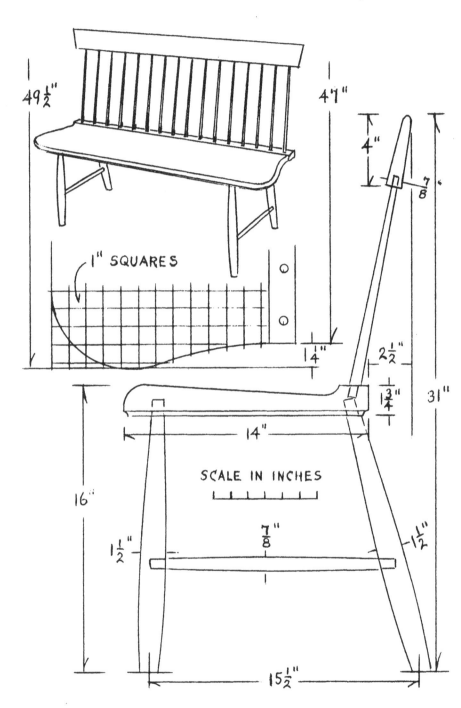

$49\frac{1}{2}"$

$47"$

$4"$

$\frac{7}{8}"$

1" SQUARES

$1\frac{1}{4}"$

$2\frac{1}{2}"$

$1\frac{3}{4}"$

$31"$

14"

SCALE IN INCHES

16"

$\frac{7}{8}"$

$1\frac{1}{2}"$

$1\frac{1}{2}"$

$15\frac{1}{2}"$

CANTERBURY SETTEE

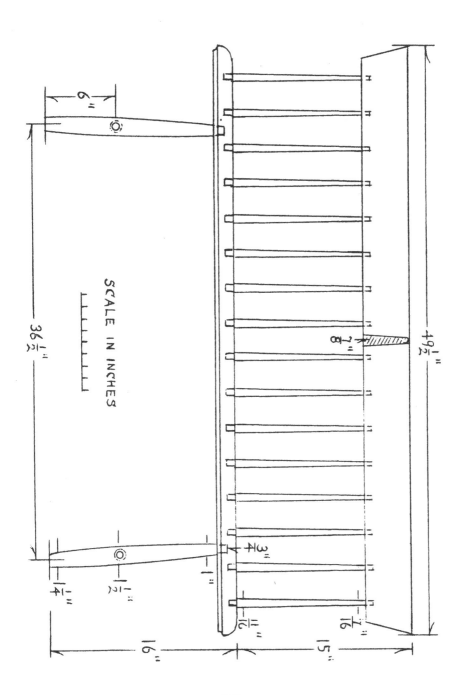

SCALE IN INCHES

63

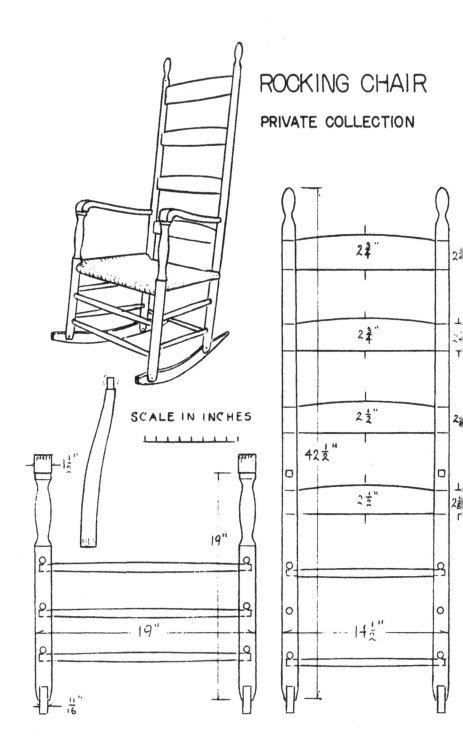

ROCKING CHAIR

PRIVATE COLLECTION

SCALE IN INCHES

$2\frac{3}{4}''$

$2\frac{3}{4}''$

$2\frac{1}{2}''$

$2\frac{1}{2}''$

$42\frac{1}{2}''$

$19''$

$19''$

$14\frac{1}{2}''$

$\frac{11}{16}''$

64

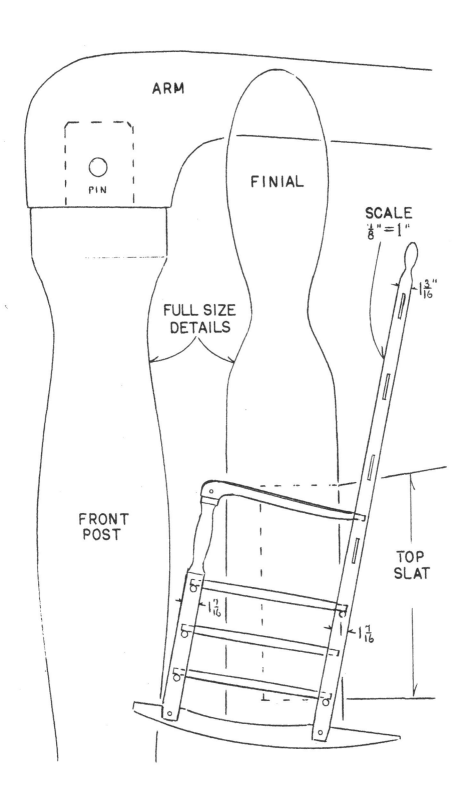

ARM

PIN

FINIAL

SCALE
$\frac{1}{8}" = 1"$

FULL SIZE
DETAILS

FRONT
POST

$1\frac{3}{16}"$

TOP
SLAT

$1\frac{7}{16}$

$1\frac{7}{16}$

65

FOOTSTOOL
HANCOCK SHAKER VILLAGE,
HANCOCK MASS.

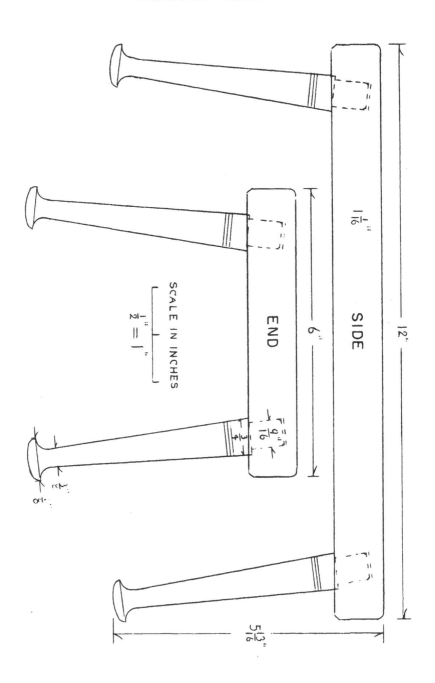

SCALE IN INCHES

$\frac{1}{2}$" = 1"

END

SIDE

$1\frac{1}{16}$"

6"

12"

$\frac{9}{16}$"

$\frac{3}{4}$"

$5\frac{13}{16}$"

FOOTSTOOL
HANCOCK SHAKER VILLAGE,
HANCOCK MASS.

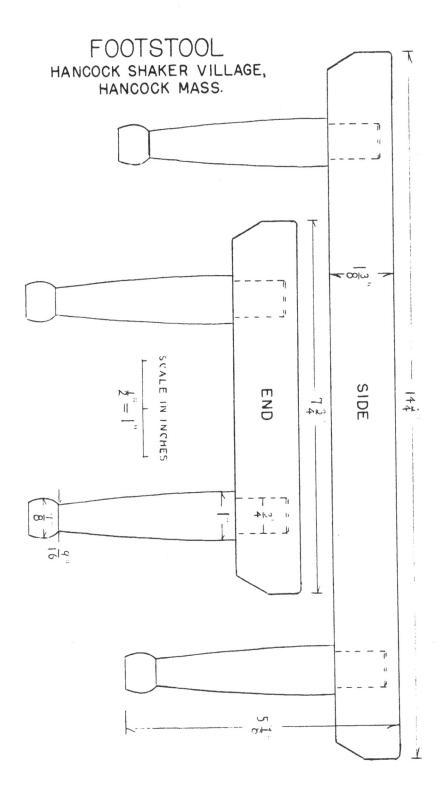

SCALE IN INCHES
$\frac{1}{2}" = 1"$

END

SIDE

$1\frac{3}{8}"$

$7\frac{3}{4}$

$11\frac{1}{4}$

$1\frac{1}{8}$

$\frac{9}{16}$

$4\frac{1}{2}$

1

$5\frac{1}{8}$

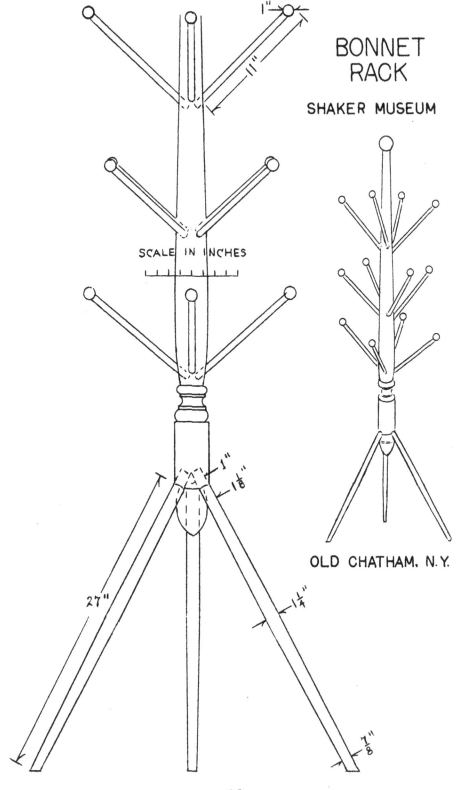

BONNET
RACK

SHAKER MUSEUM

SCALE IN INCHES

OLD CHATHAM, N.Y.

68

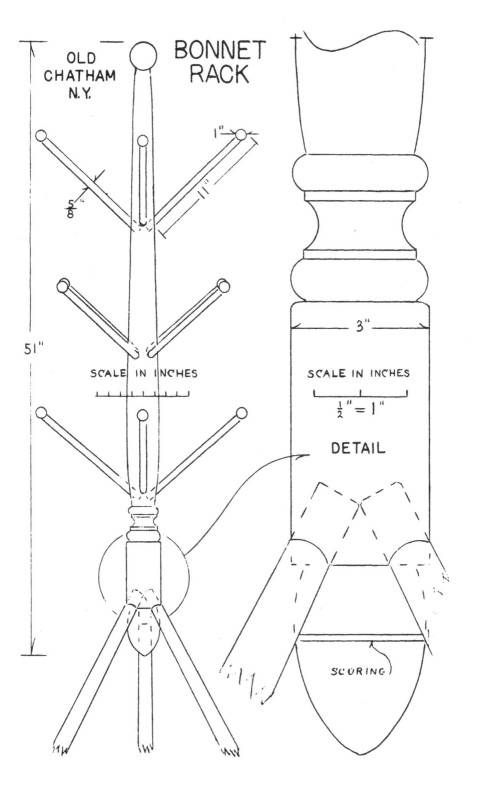

OLD
CHATHAM
N.Y.

BONNET
RACK

1"

$\frac{5}{8}$"

1"

51"

SCALE IN INCHES

3"

SCALE IN INCHES

$\frac{1}{2}$" = 1"

DETAIL

SCORING

LANTERN
THE CHATHAM MUSEUM, OLD CHATHAM, N.Y.

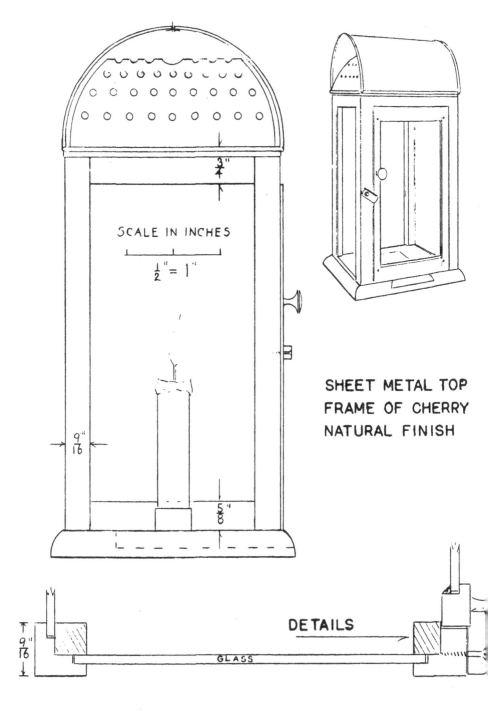

SCALE IN INCHES

$\frac{1}{2}'' = 1''$

$\frac{3}{4}''$

$\frac{9}{16}''$

$\frac{5}{8}''$

SHEET METAL TOP
FRAME OF CHERRY
NATURAL FINISH

$\frac{9}{16}''$

DETAILS

GLASS

LANTERN
THE CHATHAM MUSEUM, OLD CHATHAM, N.Y.

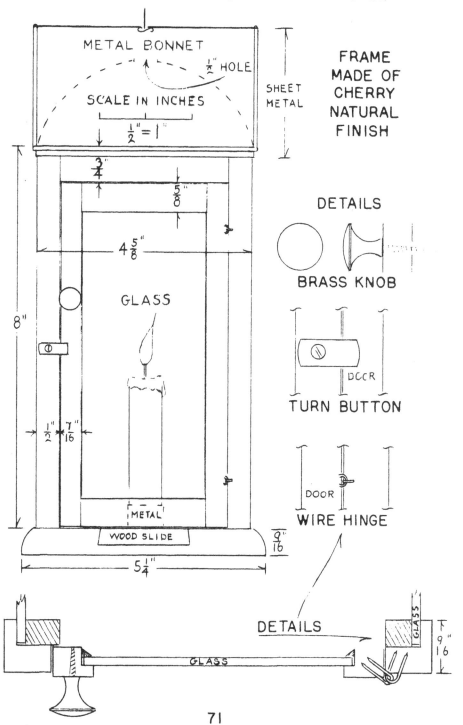

FRAME
MADE OF
CHERRY
NATURAL
FINISH

METAL BONNET

$\frac{1}{4}$" HOLE

SHEET METAL

SCALE IN INCHES

$\frac{1}{2}$" = 1"

$\frac{3}{4}$"

$\frac{5}{8}$"

$4\frac{5}{8}$"

8"

GLASS

$\frac{1}{2}$" $\frac{7}{16}$"

METAL

WOOD SLIDE

$\frac{9}{16}$"

$5\frac{1}{4}$"

DETAILS

BRASS KNOB

DOOR

TURN BUTTON

DOOR

WIRE HINGE

DETAILS

GLASS

GLASS

$\frac{9}{16}$"

MAPLE BIRCH CHERRY

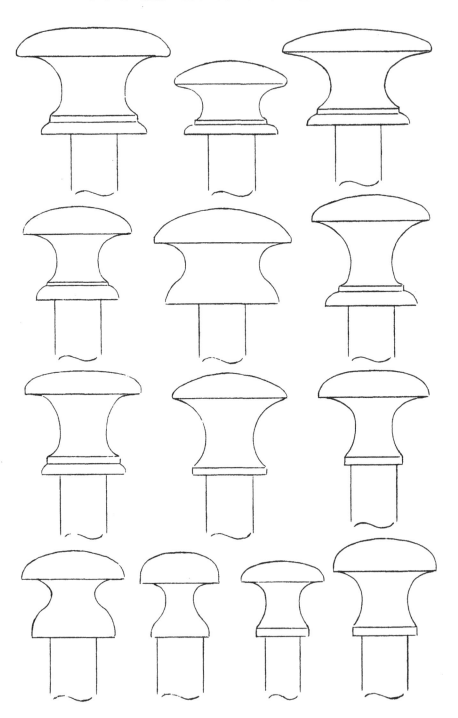

KNOBS AND PULLS

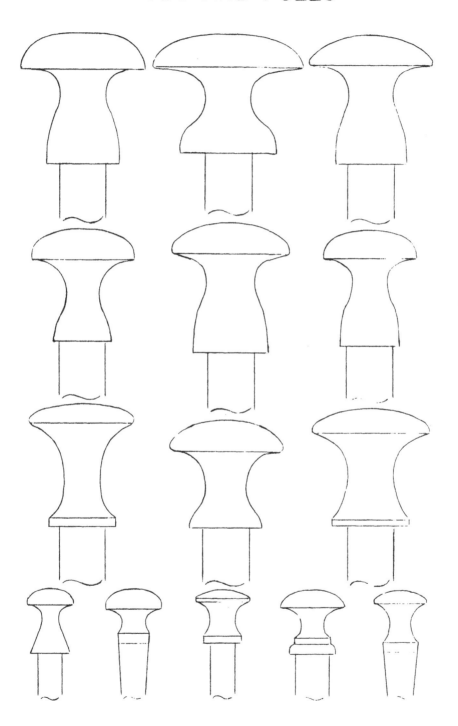

DRESSMAKER'S WEIGHT
MAPLE

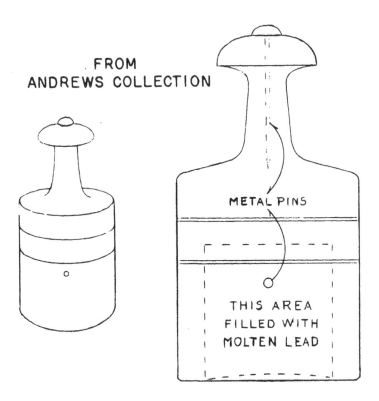

FROM
ANDREWS COLLECTION

METAL PINS

THIS AREA
FILLED WITH
MOLTEN LEAD

DARNER
CURLY MAPLE

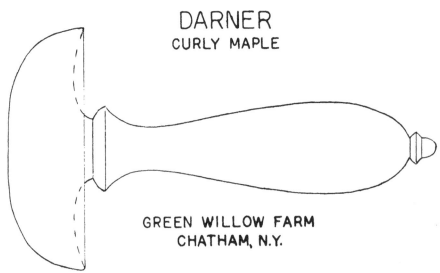

GREEN WILLOW FARM
CHATHAM, N.Y.

On the following pages are measured drawings of a secretary or fall-front desk which I made for my own use.

It follows closely the design of two original early pieces of Shaker furniture and therefore must be clearly signed and dated as a Shaker type piece of furniture. Photograph on page 84.

E.H.

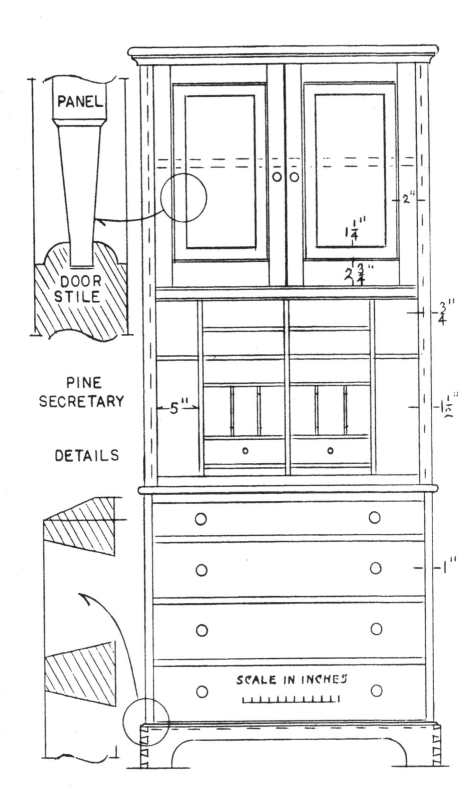

PANEL

DOOR
STILE

PINE
SECRETARY

DETAILS

5"

2"

1¼"

2¾"

¾"

1½"

1"

SCALE IN INCHES

76

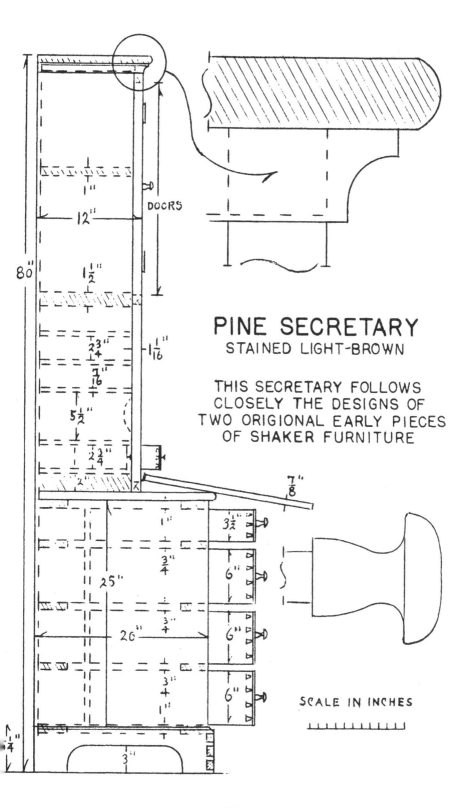

PINE SECRETARY
STAINED LIGHT-BROWN

THIS SECRETARY FOLLOWS
CLOSELY THE DESIGNS OF
TWO ORIGIONAL EARLY PIECES
OF SHAKER FURNITURE

DOORS

80"

12"

1"

1½"

2¾"

7/16"

5½"

2¾"

2"

1 1/16"

7/8"

3½"

¾"

6"

6"

25"

26"

¾"

1"

¼"

3"

SCALE IN INCHES

Dining Table — page 48

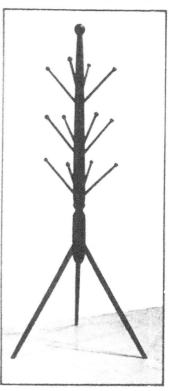

Wood Box   page 60

79

Bonnet Rack   page 68

Upright Desk—page 30

Pine Wash Stand — page 46   Case of Drawers — page 28

Storage Bench — page 22

81

Lantern — page 70

Tall Clock   page 56

82

Candlestand   page 54

Shaker Type Secretary — page 76

INDEX

ABOUT THE AUTHOR

This is the third book in the series on Shaker furniture and artifacts by Ejner Handberg.

Mr. Handberg was a skilled cabinetmaker with more than fifty years' experience who first became interested in Shaker furniture and design when people brought the valuable Shaker pieces to him to repair or restore. Born in Denmark, he came to the U.S. at 17 years of age and learned his craft from 19th-century cabinetmakers who insisted upon precision and accuracy.

Volume I and II in this series on Shaker Furniture and Woodenware each contain meticulous drawings of many different types of Shaker chairs, boxes, tables, stools, knobs, candlesticks, trays, benches and similar pieces.

Volume III includes many larger items, such as rocking chairs, tables, school desks, sewing stands, cupboards, a storage bench, a clock case, an upright desk, a dining table, a lantern, pine cupboards, a settee, and counters.

In these three books, Mr. Handberg exercised extreme care to perfect measured drawings of these original Shaker pieces for the purpose of reproducing them in his own shop. Each drawing in every book is unique because it is carefully measured from an original Shaker piece. He emulated the reverence that these unusual people had for wood and the purely functional purpose in furniture.

The informed amateur worker in wood, as well as the professional cabinetmaker and the enthusiastic collector will find Mr. Handberg's books a valuable addition to the perpetuation of Shaker qualities.